89+ Beginners' Tips

JUMP, FROGGIES!
Writing Children's Books

Edith Hope Fine

eFrog Press
Carlsbad, CA

Cover and spot art by Suzanne Santillan
Typesetting by Andrea Leljak

ISBN 13: 978-0-9894356-8-0

Library of Congress Control Number: 2015939320

www.efrogpress.com

eFrog Press
Carlsbad, CA

Beginner Tyro Novice
Rookie TRAINEE
LEARNER APPRENTICE
Greenhorn NEWCOMER

Every writer was once new.

For all who love the magical worlds of words, writing, books, and children.

EHF

CONTENTS

INTRODUCTION
Why This Book

What's the Scoop?

By the pond you spot a sign: Writing for Children. In the pond, three frogs sit on a log. One decides to jump.
How many are left on the log?

Three—because there's a difference between deciding and doing.

Writing for children.

- You've thought about it.
- Longed to know more.
- Wondered if it's for you.

But will you just decide? Or, like a daring froggy, will you jump?

Today's the day to plunge in.

You're new, but ready.
Ready to stop talking, wishing, and hoping.
Ready to leap into writing books for kids.

This book has three parts:

> I. On Your Mark! Know the Field—Quick-Start Basics
> II. Get Set! The Writing Process—From Idea to Submission
> III. Go! "We'll buy it!"—Contract, Publication, Marketing

Writing for children may seem like child's play:

- Creating amazing characters
- Inventing wild plots in fiction
- Finding sprightly, engaging ways to present facts in nonfiction

But writing for children is hard work. You must understand the process:

- Specific writing elements, such as structure, characterization, setting, and plot
- How to submit your work
- How to deal with rejection
- Your role in marketing

... and so much more.

Who Is This Book For?

This book is aimed specifically at beginning writers and people brand new to children's writing. It's your guide to building your knowledge, experience, and expertise.

People who write for children can't *not* write. Something inside pushes us to reach readers from toddlers to young adults—to make them laugh, make them cry, and lead them into worlds beyond their own.

Feel a keen fervor for the task ahead? Your goal of creating books for children is realistic.

If you follow me on Pinterest, you know I love the comics. In a great Ballard Street strip, a feisty woman in plaid Bermudas and sneakers strides fiercely forth. Her sweatshirt reads, "To hell with fear."

Fear paralyzes you, holds you back, and keeps you captive.

Feeling daunted? A little healthy trepidation is fine as you set out. But don't let it stop you. If you never go out on a limb, never make a misstep, never dare to send out a manuscript, you have the strong potential to ... lead a safe, unpublished life.

What This Book Will Do

Things are changing fast in the world of children's books and publishing. Writing for children is a huge topic. This book will take a wide-ranging look at the field and give you many specific clues. (To get the idea, take a quick look at the A to Z list of topics at the end of this book.)

Jump, Froggies! will present insights into both the magical and the mundane aspects of writing for kids. With this book, you will:

- See the big picture
- Get a jump start
- Avoid time-wasting mistakes
- Develop plans and goals
- Strengthen your writing skills
- Learn from examples (and bloopers I've made)

What This Book *Won't* Do

This book is not designed to:

- Teach you all you need to know about writing
- Tell you where to sell your manuscript
- Do the practice writing you must do to succeed
- Network for you
- Follow up on leads
- Teach you about social media
- Tell you what's wrong with your manuscript (although you'll pick up clues for strengthening your writing)
- Take classes for you
- Find your personal writing space
- Develop your writing routine

These jobs are yours.

Why Children's Books?

 Write the stories and poems and drama that will give your readers more to be human with.

— Gary D. Schmidt, two-time Newbery Honor Winner
Lizzie Bright and the Buckminster Boy, *The Wednesday Wars*, and more

Why do so many people long to write books for kids?

Perhaps because our own lives — our childhood lives and our current lives — have been deeply affected by reading.

Or because books can reach children with rough lives and fly them to places beyond.

Or help them make sense of the world.

Or learn empathy.

Or laugh out loud.

Or think in a new way.

Frank Bruni of the *New York Times* wrote this in "Read, Kids, Read": "I believe in reading—not just in its power to transport but in its power to transform." You believe in the power of books, too, or you wouldn't have picked up this book. The books you'll write can change lives.

 I don't want to write for adults. I want to write for readers who can perform miracles. Only children perform miracles when they read.

—Astrid Lindgren (1907–2002), *Pippi Longstocking*

Why Me?

I'm a veteran writer who can put you on the fast track to writing for kids. You'll get a jump start with tips, suggestions, insights, encouragement, the true scoop, and more, all based on lessons learned in my three-plus decades of writing. I'm a connector—I love linking beginners to experienced writers for a quick head start in the field.

Along with teaching writing for children for close to twenty years, I have hundreds of magazine and newspaper credits and eighteen published books. I'm a longtime member of SCBWI (the Society of Children's Book Writers and Illustrators), run the lively published members' group of our San Diego SCBWI chapter, and serve on the advisory board for UC San Diego Extension's Children's Book Writing and Children's Book Illustration certificate programs.

Every week I get emails, calls, and queries from people like you seeking quick answers to huge questions:

> "I've finished my children's book. Where shall I get it published?"
> "Can you help me get an illustrator?"
> "Do I have to know what age my book is for? All kids will love it."
> "My child's class loves my book. What now?"
> "Could I buy you coffee and you can tell me how to market my book?"

"My little picture book about the talking stop sign is done. Do I need an agent?"

"I have a children's book idea. You can write it and we'll split the money."

"My neighbor's daughter wants to write books. Could you call her?"

Sound familiar?

How about a jump start? In a couple of paragraphs I can cover questions, topics, or techniques that took me years to figure out when I was new to the field. You'll also learn from my errors and false starts.

What to Look For: The Format

These icons will guide you.

FAQ _____

FAQs (frequently asked questions), like this one:

You: How do I find an illustrator for my picture book?
Me: You don't.
(That's the truth. More anon.)

> ## TIP
>
> Look for quick tips in these shaded boxes.

 Quotes from published authors, with book titles and links to their sites and blogs when available.

 **ALPHY SAYS**

"Watch for me, Alphy, the microcyanosaurus from Edith's Cryptomania! I'll pop in occasionally with sage advice."

Froggy Thumbs Up and Thumbs Down cues for "Do this, not that."

IN YOUR JOURNAL Ideas for you to write, track, and try.

Your Writing Journal

You need just one thing to get started: a journal. It doesn't matter what you use—a yellow notepad, a three-ring notebook, or a computer document—as long as it's dedicated to staking out your path to children's writing.

In your journal you'll keep track of your progress and discoveries. In it, you'll record:

> Goals
>
> Children's books and authors
>
> Ideas
>
> Questions
>
> Tips
>
> Notes
>
> Leads
>
> Cool words
>
> Grammar and usage tips
>
> . . . and more

Set up your journal now. When you come to a writing prompt, act on it. By the time you've finished this book, you'll have your own personal how-to manual.

TIP

First tip: Don't be overwhelmed.

If your journey into writing for children seems too huge to tackle, read Anne Lamott's *Bird by Bird*. Her brother, stunned by his homework —a huge bird report due for school—got this sage advice from their dad: "Take it bird by bird."

You'll do the same. You won't learn all you need to know in an instant. Start with a single aspect of writing for children—one that pulls you in. Then, like the three little pigs, build your knowledge and skills brick by brick.

PART I

On Your Mark!

Know the Field—Quick-Start Basics

CHAPTER 1

The Big Picture

Let's Begin

FAQ _____

You: How do I get started?

Me: You start by starting. This isn't an eating contest where you have to wolf down eighty-nine chicken wings in ten minutes. You'll take small, tasty bites—eighty-nine (plus!) tips on writing for children.

You can read this guide front to back or hop to subjects that catch your eye.

Be savvy as you begin your exploration of writing for children:

- Come across a term you don't know? Check the Internet.
- Writing a middle grade novel (MG)? You need to be devouring a stack of current MGs.
- Ready to quit with your first rejection? Holy schmoley, Batman. Don't.

TIP

Get your domain name now. I own both Edith Fine (www.edithfine.com) and Edith Hope Fine (www.edithhopefine.com). Go to a domain registration service or check with your webhosting company. If your name is fairly common, distinguish it from others with the same moniker by adding "author" or "books" or "writes" or "4kids" to your name. Be sure to renew when the time comes. You don't want to lose your domain name once you're established.

Misconceptions

George Gershwin's famed "It Ain't Necessarily So" can apply to writing, too:

> Publishers will help you with spelling and punctuation.
> Children's books are easy to write.
> You can earn a great living writing for children.

I'll share simple truths. If you think you can hand imperfect manuscripts over to editors for fixing, that writing for children is as easy as ABC, or that you'll make a lot of money in this profession, you'd better start belting "It Ain't Necessarily So."

Writing for kids isn't like sailing glassy seas. Don your wet-weather gear. Your future holds everything from calm harbors to storms and whirlpools.

To Be a Writer . . .

Writers are:

- Lifelong learners
- Curious
- Open to new ideas
- Listeners
- Determined
- Worker bees
- Patient
- Striving
- Eager
- Observers
- Creative

Look at a person, a vehicle, or a building and attempt to notice things you know others have missed. How many details can you describe? What doesn't fit? What patterns do you see? What do you think you know based on a quick glance and your gut reaction? The more you do this, the better you get.

— Lee Silber, the Creative Person series and more
(www.leesilber.com)

Successful children's writers do notice things—everything from hummingbird eggs in a tiny nest outside a window to a gorgeous sunset. We watch how people move, laugh, speak. We read to learn how others think, react, and keep their secrets. We love words. We listen to conversations. We wonder about people's jobs, people's roles in families, other cultures, faraway places.

Do you share these characteristics?

TIP

Many beginners shy away from using the word "writer." Start using it now:

"I drive for UPS and I'm a writer."
"I'm a nurse and a writer."
"I teach English and I'm a writer."

IN YOUR JOURNAL

Know this puzzle? Copy these dots in your newly minted journal. Without lifting your pencil, link all nine evenly-spaced dots with four straight lines.

● ● ●

● ● ●

● ● ●

Give it a whirl before checking out the solution on page 162.

To solve this puzzle you must literally think outside the box. Now, think figuratively outside the box to get your writing career rolling. Write down three steps you can take this week.

Ideas to get you started:

Meet with a children's librarian.

Volunteer to read to kids at your local elementary school.

Write about your latest trip for your local paper; include photos and travel tips.

Borrow a book on a specific aspect of writing, such as viewpoint or character.

Learn one new word a day (www.wordsmith.org).

Google one aspect of writing or grammar that's puzzling to you.

Submit greeting card ideas for people with your sense of humor.

Write a kid-friendly magazine piece about a hobby of yours.

Attend a local Society of Children's Book Writers and
 Illustrators meeting.

Find or start a writing group.

Write a fan letter to your favorite author.

Do short daily journal entries.

Enter a writing contest.

The Truth About Time

FAQ

You: How long will it take for me to see my name in print?
Me: Hey, check a crystal ball!

Time is weird. Slow as pulled taffy. Gone in a finger snap.

The time it will take you—an unpublished writer—to be published is unpredictable. A humor piece about the surprise spraying you got when a cactus spike pierced your brand- new "As Seen on TV" hose could hit your local newspaper next week.

If you get a gig writing a newspaper column as I did, you'll be published weekly.

With a work-for-hire project (payment is a set fee; no royalties), you're on a tight deadline and using a given format; you could see a book within the year.

You could work for a decade on your YA novel. It's accepted. Yay. But editing, copyediting, proofing, graphic design, cover and spot art, actual printing, plus unforeseen hiccups along the way could eat up three more years.

The road to becoming a published writer can be long, but if you stay determined, keep learning, strive to make your writing stronger and stronger, and practice, practice, practice, it's a matter of *when*, not *if*.

You may wonder, too, about the chances of a newbie's scoring big-time with a first book. It can happen. In truth, the odds against this lovely phenomenon are astronomical. Most writers spend years learning their craft, sending out manuscripts, and getting rejections before their first book sale.

A couple of "time" tales:

Tale One

In the early 1990s, I invented a grumpy cricket for a new take on the Christmas story, but for the life of me could not find a buyer and put the manuscript away. Years later, when Boyds Mills Press bought it, the editor and I tweaked one small section. It was virtually the same piece I'd tried to sell years earlier.

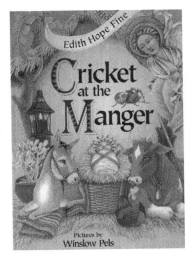

Tale Two

For years I worked on a manuscript I'd dubbed *Yawn Around Town*. I had a refrain: "Yawn around, yawn around the sleepytime town." I made numerous stabs at finding the story (including the truly awful idea of a talking yawn). My *Yawn* file bulged. And whatever the new angle, this manuscript came in at 1000+ words.

Then speakers at our 2010 San Diego SCBWI conference stressed their love of short, tight manuscripts. I went home and hacked away at *Yawn*. Two decades after I had the original idea, the drastically shortened manuscript caught the eye and ear of an agent. She and I sent the manuscript back and forth. I parked my nose in a rhyming dictionary for months, found words to conjure up fresh images, and ironed out wrinkles in rhythm and rhyme until the words fit together as snugly as jigsaw puzzle pieces. Now the 132 words meld with luminous nighttime illustrations by artist Christopher Denise in *Sleepytime Me*.

TIP

Did you catch "in the early 1990s" and "two decades" in these tales? Stay realistic. Give yourself time.

Know Your Young Audience

 Do you have an imaginary friend? You should! One of the most overlooked things in writing for children is children. Seems crazy, but it's often true. Many writers forget the child reader and create stories that aren't going to entertain a child because they are too long or too dull or too adult. Children want to see action, surprises, playfulness, emotional intensity, and energetic characters. Writers who really work at making their stories engaging and satisfying for children are more likely to succeed with grown-ups like agents and editors. When you sit down to write, make room for an imaginary child reader right next to you.

— Andrea Zimmerman, *Eliza's Cherry Trees: Japan's Gift to America, Dig!,* and more
Blog: *Picture Book Party* (www.picturebookparty.com)

Your goal is to write for children. You'd better know what kids and teens are like as well as what they like.

You teach preschool or seventh grade or high school? Work at a Boys & Girls Club? Teach swimming classes? Lead a Girl Scout troop? Teach chemistry to teens? Dance with toddlers at the library? You're a nanny? A coach? A school secretary? You have energetic kids, nieces and nephews, grandchildren, neighbors?

Being around the audience you're writing for gives you a leg up.

You must know what today's kids wear, eat, talk about, and sound like if your work is contemporary. Whatever the time period, you need to know young people's consuming interests and what makes them laugh. You must be in tune with the inner lives of real children: the angst, drama, stumbles, hopes, and dreams.

This firsthand knowledge layers your manuscripts and deepens your characters. No stilted dialogue for you. No perfectly behaved darlings who lack flaws. Two-dimensional, stereotypical kids won't stand a chance of wheedling their way into your manuscripts.

A First Writing Prompt

> *Everything I write comes from my childhood in one way or another. I am forever drawing on the sense of mystery and wonder and possibility that pervaded that time of my life.*

> —Kate DiCamillo, National Ambassador for Young People's Literature (2014–2015) and two-time Newbery Award winner; *Bink and Gollie, Flora & Ulysses, The Magician's Elephant*, and more (www.katedicamillo.com)

Dig deep into your past. Remember what it was like to be a kid.

In Your Journal

Hop into your trusted time machine and write from your own childhood. Use one of these prompts or think of your own:

- A time you got lost
- A food you hated
- An accident
- The Tooth Fairy
- A pet's funeral
- A fight
- Your favorite book
- A recess incident
- Halloween
- A favorite toy or game
- A first kiss
- Lying and getting away with it
- Your first bra or jock strap
- A trip
- A big fear
- A hilarious family anecdote

Be a Pro—Join a Professional Group

If you're brand new to writing, there are groups you can join for support: Mystery Writers of America, Poetry Society of America, Writers Guild of America. But there's only one organization specifically for us—people who write for children. That's the Society of Children's Book Writers and Illustrators (SCBWI), an international organization cofounded by prolific children's writers Lin Oliver and Stephen Mooser.

SCBWI membership gives you access to loads of resources: awards and grants, an event calendar, Lee Wind's official SCBWI blog (www.scbwi.blogspot.com), conference info, and more. As a member, you have access to *THE BOOK: The Essential Guide to Publishing for Children*, located in the Resource Library section of the SCBWI website. This three hundred-page book contains answers to your pressing questions—everything from formatting your manuscript to legal issues. Members can also order a hard copy.

The *SCBWI Bulletin* is a bimonthly publication loaded with info for children's writers. As a member, you can access the archives. (This is also found in the Resource Library section of the website.) Read the "People" section to see who's publishing what. Look at their titles. Be amused by the sound of a paper page turning when you flip through the newsletter. (Makes me smile.)

Also check out Verla Kay's Blueboard, a message and chat board for members.

Across the US and internationally, writers gather at SCBWI events. Find the regional chapter nearest you (www.scbwi.org; click on Regional Chapters). SCBWI chapters vary in size and scope and your local chapter may be a long drive away. If so, pick and choose your activities and make connections by email and other social media, like SCBWI's LinkedIn page.

Early on, I got active in the San Diego chapter. I'm glad I did. So hop in. Lend a hand, even if it's moving chairs for a meeting. You'll learn more, make connections, and go further faster.

If possible, attend local chapter meetings. Glean as much information as you can. Early in my teaching days, a mentor said of presentations and meetings, "Be happy if you get one gem. Then use it." I still remember the SCBWI conference where Dav Pilkey told us the funniest word in the English language: underpants!

Our active San Diego chapter holds monthly meetings and offers a monthly newsletter, help with finding a writing group (also called a critique group), timely information, yearly conferences or retreats, a sub-group for published members, and more.

Each year, the first weekend of August, SCBWI hosts a major conference in Los Angeles for what Lin Oliver calls "a meeting of the tribe." Members attend from around the US and the world for outstanding speakers, inspiration, connections, resources, heaps of books to graze through, smaller presentations on specific topics, sessions especially for beginners, and informal chats over a glass of wine with new friends.

The words and wisdom of the keynote speakers are fuel for your fire. There is nothing like being in a huge room with fellow bibliophiles who care deeply about young readers and their futures. You have the opportunity to speak with the "big names" in children's writing, like these authors who have spoken at recent conferences: Patricia MacLachlan, Gary D. Schmidt, Ruta Sepetys, Karen Cushman, Gary Paulsen, Laurie Halse Anderson, Jon Scieszka, Richard Peck, David Wiesner, Meg Medina, Judy Blume, and many others.

You can pay for one-on-one critiques of your unpublished manuscripts.

Side note: Artists can submit portfolios of their work, with the top six getting mentorships.

At the 2012 conference, I sat with 2011 illustrator mentorship winner Alice Ratterree and Brian Won, a first-time conference-goer, at Melissa Sweet's marvelous breakout session for artists. Imagine our excitement when Brian received a 2012 mentorship award that evening! His website notes, "Brian speaks softly and carries a Ticonderoga #2." I love that. He's got *voice*. Watch Brian's *Hooray for Hat!* trailer (www.brianwon.com).

Conference no-nos: Don't hog a speaker during a session. Ask broad questions that will benefit the whole audience. (Not: "Do you think my mouse should go to the fair or head to the river to help his friends?") The same goes for after a presentation. A ten-minute discussion is not okay when there's a line of people wanting to touch base with the speaker. Never (*never*) hand a manuscript to an agent or editor on the spot. (Exception: unless personally invited!)

SCBWI offers conference suggestions for first-timers. Soak up that information before you arrive. Study the program ahead of time. Go prepared with specific goals. Read and study books by speakers. Write down questions to ask. Mark the speeches and breakout sessions that sound intriguing and helpful. Skip events not relevant to you. Consider attending one of the intensives offered on the fourth day of the conference for a full day with an expert in a small group of fellow writers. (These fill fast. Know the date conference registration opens and sign up ASAP.)

At the conference, take good notes. Add your own comments to posts at the conference blog. Get involved. I met Brooke Bessesen, founder of Authors for Earth Day (A4ED), at an SCBWI conference. Check out the site (www. authorsforearthday.org) and read my blog post (www.authorsforearthday. org/edith-fine) about the fun I had doing a big A4ED gig and raising money for the San Elijo Lagoon Conservancy. You never know whom you'll meet in the halls or elevators or pool or at the gala Saturday night costume party. You could make friendships that will last a lifetime.

Check out past conferences at the SCBWI website so you know what to expect. The annual conference may seem expensive—registration, hotel, travel, food, and extras. But think of it like a series of focused classes. When you lay the groundwork and plan carefully, it's more than worthwhile. The weekend is exhilarating and exhausting, but you can always recharge with chocolate or your favorite treat in your room. If you're working at your craft and submitting work, the expenses could be tax deductible.

TIP

Join SCBWI. Check out the many SCBWI grants and their guidelines—the list of grants offered to members keeps growing. Don't just think about applying. Follow through with an application.

Contests and grants are a great way to break into the children's publishing market. I entered two stories in Highlights for Children's annual contest. While I didn't win, the editors read my story, liked it, and published it the following year. And know that SCBWI offers new writers several work-in-progress grants *to apply for.*

—Debra Schmidt, assistant regional advisor, SCBWI San Diego

Read, Read, Read

 Read like a wolf eats, read when they tell you not to read, and read what they tell you not to read. Read all the time, and turn the television off.

— Gary Paulsen, author of *Hatchet, Soldier's Heart,* and more

If you want to write for kids, you must read kids' books. Must.

Bibliophiles have a leg up when writing for children. Stored in the attic boxes of the mind are years of syntax, vocabulary, rhythm, glorious plots and characters, intriguing settings, and heart-stopping moments.

Voracious reading makes you more discerning and helps you sort the moving, endearing books from the dismal dreck.

So, read. Broadly. Deeply. Books for adults. Books for children and teens. Magazines, newspapers, comics, puzzles, the works. Determined to write chapter books? Devour them. Intrigued by science fantasy? Know what's out there.

Visit your local library often. Hover over the children's bookshelves. Befriend the librarian at your nearest elementary school. Stop by on a Friday afternoon, sign out a stack of books, dive into them over the weekend, and return them on Monday morning so they're available to the students.

You can still love the classics from your childhood. At the 2012 SCBWI conference, Jon Klassen (who became a Caldecott Award winner five months later) said of a childhood favorite, "You [revisit it] because you still have a crush on it . . . It's walking just ahead of you."

 When you reread a classic, you do not see more in the book than you did before; you see more in yourself than there was before.

— Clifton Fadiman (1904–1999), editor and critic

Fadiman's words hold true for our readers and for ourselves. But it's also important that you know what's being published today for young readers.

Learn From What You Read

When you read children's books, you store marvels in the hidden reaches of your brain. When you turn to your own writing, the lessons you've learned from these authors subconsciously rise to the fore. Go to the geniuses to learn. The Robert Newton Pecks. The Cynthia Voigts. The Karen Hesses. The Kate DiCamillos. The Markus Zusaks. And so many others. Look for the books that move you to tears, make you laugh aloud, give you food for thought . . . learn from these books and their writers.

 Have a writing role model – a successful children's author whose work and career you admire. When I first started writing for children, I chose Cynthia Rylant. She writes for all ages from picture book to middle grade novel, easy reader to poetry. Her credo is "All I need is peacefulness and postage." I love her work. Because of her early success, she was able to experiment and follow every interesting idea. Having this writing "idol" gave me a vision for the kind of work I wanted to do and the kind of *writer's life I wanted.*

—Jodie Shull, author of *Words of Promise: A Story about James Weldon Johnson*, **and more**

Read actively. Playwright and screenwriter Lucy Alibar of *Beasts of the Southern Wild* says she'll "read an Alice Munro short story, and then I'll reread it to see, so mechanically, how in the last two paragraphs she just reaches into your heart and pulls it out, like Indiana Jones."

Starting now, be a double reader like Alibar. Read first for pleasure. Absorb the deliciousness. Be transported. Marvel at the mystery. Revel in fabulous writing. Then turn around and read to learn. Note how each author accomplishes the following:

- Builds tension
- Gives characters depth
- Slows the pace
- Handles transitions
- Makes your heart beat faster
- Lets you feel smart when you know something the protagonist doesn't yet know
- Brings tears to your eyes

- Creates an eerie but believable setting
- Travels through time
- Unfolds the plot
- Names the characters
- Makes you laugh aloud
- Leaves you wanting more

Watch for the power in the structure:

- Fresh or startling similes and metaphors
- Powerful, specific verbs
- The rhythm of a phrase, sentence, or paragraph
- A clever, unexpected plot turn
- How an era is evoked
- Why you felt as though you'd fallen inside the story, experiencing it yourself
- What made you turn the pages fast or read until two a.m.
- A clue imbedded in the beginning
- Great examples of show, don't tell
- Sensory details
- Clever analogies in nonfiction that make complex ideas clear
- A theme in a biography that's realized in every chapter

IN YOUR JOURNAL

From today on, in the "Children's Books and Authors" section of your journal, you'll track your reading in the field. For each book, note the title, author, publisher, date of publication, length, number of chapters, number of pages, and age level. Give yourself a short synopsis, plus some highlights to help you remember that book: something that made you think or something that gave you a mini-lesson in writing for children.

 If you want to write children's books, then you need to be a reader, supporter, and buyer of children's books. Just as you would never apply for a position as a rocket scientist without knowing rocket science, you can't be a children's book author without knowing children's books. Do yourself a favor and get thee to the children's books section of your local library or, even better, a bookstore.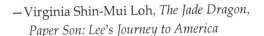

— Virginia Shin-Mui Loh, *The Jade Dragon,*
   Paper Son: Lee's Journey to America

Write What You Know

"Write what you know" may sound counterintuitive. "Hey, my life isn't that interesting," you may be thinking. What this phrase means is "find fodder in your life." Mine your past—your own singular experiences.

This does *not* mean recording things precisely as they happened!

The garden lady in my book *Water, Weed, and Wait* is Miss Marigold. She and Mr. Barkley give the students their own marigold seeds to plant. This all came from the deep past when I was teaching gifted kids in Manhattan Beach. I taught the gardening group, and at one point had students pull marigold seeds from what looked like dead, shriveled, brown pods. Little did I know this marigold secret would appear in a book forty years later!

When my sons were lads, we often took stale bread to feed the ducks at a nearby lagoon. We could spot the greedy ones. We made sure the laggards got their share. We knew the sensory stuff—the feel of pulling bread apart, the sounds of flapping and skrawks and splashed landings, the sight of the flock strutting boldly to us and the wide stretch of water, the pungent scents. We were immersed in the experience. We knew duck-feeding. We could be in the duck-feeding moment whether with the ducks or not. I could easily write about it.

But duck feeding alone isn't strong enough to sustain a scene.

The lightbulb "write what you know" moment came for me while reading a children's book where a girl feeding ducks meets a Vietnam vet sitting on the dock. Duck details splashed their way into the writing, interspersed with dialogue that moved the story forward. The scene was pitch-perfect.

Think layering. Do you ski? Have you thrown up on a plane? Fed a baby? Dropped your keys down the gutter? Are you a football fan? Great at Hula-Hooping? Terrific! Build on your own unique set of interests, skills, experiences—what you know!—to create believable scenes that come fully to life for your readers.

Consider what's unique in your life. My belief in teleporting (ha!) and my love of Greek and Latin roots (passed down by my dad) combined when I tackled *Cryptomania!* Another story could grow from the WWII letters sent by my uncle, a soldier stationed in France, to my aunt. For now, they're just stewing at the back of my brainbox. The key? People know the war in a general way, but no one else has these particular old letters.

IN YOUR JOURNAL

Take two minutes to jot down ten things from your own life you could weave into a story. You really know . . . hockey, mountain trails, apartment living, woodworking . . . you get the idea. Don't shy away from life's darker moments. Our readers need to know their own hearts — deeply felt personal moments can let them know they're not alone.

Explore: Beyond Books, Different Styles

 Don't keep your writing aspirations a secret. Several years ago, I shared my writing goals with a coworker. She became a content developer for an online education company, and remembering that I was an aspiring writer, she offered me a write-for-hire job. Later, a critique group friend was hired by Disney English and gave my name to the project manager. This led to my second write-for-hire position.

—Debra Schmidt, assistant regional advisor, SCBWI San Diego

As a beginner, any writing you do counts. I did a lot of non-book writing to establish myself and gain credits. Some of it even made money.

You could start with recapping robotics meetings for parents, writing a craft piece for your local paper, or editing a newsletter for a favorite organization. I used newsletters I'd written for my AAUW branch as writing evidence to get my weekly newspaper column.

Follow a deep interest. Since Judith Josephson and I see and hear grammar bloopers everywhere, we now write a monthly Grammar Patrol post for the eFrog Press blog. (See www.efrogpress.com, Blog: Take the Leap, Grammar and Usage. Use the drop-down menu for specific topics.) The tone is informal, chatty. We focus on specific topics, another way to let families, students, and teachers know about our handy *Nitty-Gritty Grammar* guides.

I've also written student workbooks. *Can-do Cursive* (www.hwtears.com) with

ɔr Jan Olsen, covers handwriting, grammar, Greek and Latin roots,
ˈiting. The other, *Greek and Latin Roots for Cryptomaniacs!*, pairs with
ɔ, ...:ania! *Teleporting into Greek and Latin with the CryptoKids.*

You can also try writing styles new to you. When Lee & Low Books started
their Bebop Books imprint, I read the guidelines and had fun concocting twelve
short manuscripts, just thirty to fifty words long. They bought one, called
Snapshots, and it's been selling since in English and Spanish. These books for
beginners are sold in sets. The royalties aren't huge, but they are handy for
expenses like toner and other office supplies and they get you a writing credit.

FAQ _____

You: What's a writing credit?
Me: A credit is your byline, the "By *Your Name*" at the top or end of a piece.

I wrote for newspapers and magazines before focusing on credits in the
children's field. I've written rebuses, science experiments, puzzles, stories,
and columns for kids' magazines and newspapers. Build your credits with
contest wins, children's magazines, the kids' page in your local paper. Work
published with your byline provides proof of your writing skills and a clue to
your writing voice.

TIP

Use Google or the *SCBWI Bulletin* to find writing contests to enter. They
could be run by local organizations, children's magazines (like *Highlights for
Children*), or children's book publishers (Lee & Low Books holds an annual
contest for writers of color). Whether you win or not is beside the point.
You're submitting your work. Contests can also provide a way in the door
at a publishing house. As always, to catch an editor's eye send only your
best work.

Newbery, Caldecott, Printz Prize—Oh My!

FAQ _____

You: What's the difference between the Caldecott and the Newbery awards?
Me: The Caldecott is for best **art**. The Newbery (spelled with one **r**, *not*
     "Newberry") is for best **writing**. The "a" and "w" are your mnemonics:
     art, **w**riting. Winners are announced in January by the American Library
     Association (www.ala.org, Awards and Grants).

As a newbie, your job is not to aim for a Newbery. Your job is learning to make your work worthy of the lovely, albeit unlikely, chance of winning this coveted award.

While your current focus is on craft, not prizes, here's an overview.

As you explore prizes in children's literature, you'll discover the Michael Printz Award, the Coretta Scott King Award, and the Robert F. Sibert Informational Book Medal, to name a few of the standouts. The American Library Association offers awards such as the Stonewall Book Awards (in the GLBT—gay, lesbian, bisexual, transgender—category) and the Margaret A. Edwards Award (honoring an author and his or her body of work).

SCBWI alone has the Golden Kite, the Crystal Kite (member choice awards), the Sid Fleischman Humor Award, the Magazine Merit Award, the Sue Alexander Award, the Jane Yolen Mid-List Author Grant, the Book Launch Award, Work-in-Progress Grants, the Promising Manuscript Award, the Martha Weston Grant, the Emerging Voices Award (to foster the emergence of diverse voices in children's book), and the Spark Award (for works created through nontraditional publishing).

Note that many states have their own awards. Judith and I were thrilled when *Armando and the Blue Tarp School* was nominated for a California Young Reader Medal, given by the California Reading Association (CRA). CRA's Eureka! Nonfiction Children's Book Award puts top-notch nonfiction squarely in the spotlight.

Getting lists of current and past winners of these prestigious prizes is easy online. Your children's librarian will also have lists of awardees and can recommend favorites for your reading list. Personally, I adore *From the Mixed-Up Files of Mrs. Basil E. Frankweiler* by the brilliant E. L. Konigsburg.

Hie yourself to the library for some of these award-winning books. Note their quality, appeal, and wide-ranging voices in both fiction and nonfiction.

In Your Journal

How many of the children's book awards just mentioned do you know?

Make two columns.

First header: Awards I Know
Second header: Need to Know More

Jot your discoveries on national and state awards and the impact of these standout books on your writing. Pledge to read one a week.

CHAPTER 2

What's Your Genre?

Home on the Range

The range of children's books is wide and deep.

Where will you park your writing skills? Will you specialize or try many genres? Your own reading may help you decide.

Some writers, like Mary Pearson and Jean Ferris, focus exclusively on young adult (YA) novels. Kathleen Krull writes engaging nonfiction. Others, like Eve Bunting, Cynthia Rylant, and Jane Yolen, have tapped many genres in the children's field—from toddler to YA.

First, know the main genres. Your local librarian can help you choose top-notch current titles as you explore the broad range.

Board Books

Think drool, rips, smudges, and toy truck rollovers and you'll know why board books have thick durable pages for chewing and running over with toy trucks. These books for toddlers are short, clear, focused. Daily life, simple concepts, engaging illustrations. Get a taste with board books by Sandra Boynton or Helen Oxenbury. These books are more expensive to produce and are often versions of an already-published book by a well-known author. Not your best starting point.

Picture Books

Fully illustrated, many picture books are first read aloud to youngsters. Kids then mimic the story, turning pages on their own, blithely telling their own delightful version. Picture book classics will draw new audiences for decades with a story that rings true. With this illustrated genre, author and artist share royalties. Few words, heart-tapping plots, twist endings. Page count is usually thirty-two. Picture books for older children may have longer word counts and address more challenging topics. Read Eve Bunting's *Fly Away Home*, about a homeless dad and son living in an airport, and *The Wall*, about a boy searching for his grandfather's name at the Vietnam Veterans Memorial Wall. (It's hard to get through this poignant book without choking up.)

Easy Readers

When the magic happens and kids begin to read for themselves, they'll grab easy readers. Reading success is important for these eager youngsters, so write focused, short manuscripts; no gigantic words or complex concepts. Many publishing houses offer these books, often written in-house or by "name" authors. Check out titles in Candlewick's Brand New Readers series and Random House's Step Into Reading series for examples.

Chapter Books

These books feature chapters, a big deal for young readers striking out on their own. The stories stay focused and the endings are strong. Check out Arnold Lobel's classic Frog and Toad books with their humor, and kid-like characters and predicaments. Upbeat, fun, sweet.

Middle Grade (MG)

With MG, you'll find engaging plots, now with subplots, for kids eight to twelve. Many just make kids giggle. Mysteries, friendship stories, adventure, silliness. Norton Juster's *The Phantom Tollbooth* and Madeleine L'Engle's *A Wrinkle in Time* are brilliant classics. If you haven't read Kate DiCamillo's *Because of Winn-Dixie*, put it at the top of your reading list. For early middle grade, check out Megan McDonald's comical Judy Moody series.

Young Adult (YA)

The YA genre is aimed at teens. The main characters are usually slightly older than the readers. You'll find more serious themes, more violence, true love, and maybe even some sex. Classics like *To Kill a Mockingbird*, *Fahrenheit 451*, *The Giver*, and *The Lord of the Rings* may come to mind. Also explore *The Hunger Games*, *The Fault in Our Stars*, *Yaqui Delgado Wants to Kick Your Ass*, and the amazing *The Book Thief*.

New Adult (NA)

For more on this emerging category aimed at older teens and young twenties, check out Deborah Halverson's *Writing New Adult Fiction* from Writer's Digest Books with insights into new adult novels with eighteen- to twenty-five-year-old characters.

> # TIP
>
> If you do focus on one genre, dive into books on writing, even ones aimed at specific genres other than children's writing. Even though I don't write mysteries, I found Chris Roerden's *Don't Murder Your Mystery: 24 Fiction-Writing Techniques to Save Your Manuscript from Turning Up D.O.A.* both amusing and helpful.

In Your Journal

Check this list, then record the genres and subgenres that click with you. For clues about where your writing interests lie, note whether your list is broad or narrow.

> Biography
> Board Books
> Chapter Books
> Easy Readers
> Fantasy
> Gateway Fantasy (Time Travel)
> Historical Fiction
> How-To
> Humor
> Horror
> GLBT (Gay, Lesbian, Bisexual, Transgender)
> Middle Grade

Multicultural
Mystery
New Adult
Novels in Verse
Poetry
Religious
Retold Fairy Tales
Science
Science Fantasy
Science Fiction
Tween (older than MG; young teens)
Young Adult

F or NF? That Is the Question

Will you opt to focus on fiction or nonfiction? Pulled in both directions? Do both. Whatever you decide, write riveting books. As you review these genres, go to your strengths first. After you've had success playing your strongest suit, stretch into other areas you find intriguing.

I've written both fiction and nonfiction. And what do we even call *Cryptomania!*? I joke at school assemblies that it's "friction." Everything about the Greek and Latin roots is true, true, true—utterly nonfiction. The teleporting, the wild adventures, the characters and critters—so very fictional.

Whether nonfiction or fiction, your writing must pop off the pages to pull in both an editor and young readers.

Nonfiction

From cells to sequoias, kids want and need information. With nonfiction, you're either an expert in your topic or you become a temporary expert. You may be able to home in on topics young readers want to explore by using expertise gained from your day job.

Wendy Perkins is a walking encyclopedia on animals. A staff writer for the San Diego Zoo's ZOONOOZ magazine, Wendy brings a love of animals and a wealth of information to her articles. (You'll know hers by her clever titles.) She's also used this expertise to write nonfiction animal books for education publishers.

With her love of nature, Caroline Arnold has written many delicious nonfiction books. She's doubly talented. Check out her cut paper illustrations (www.carolinearnoldportfolio.blogspot.com). Caroline has also created clever art projects kids can do that relate to her books—another idea for when your own books are published.

Nonfiction books provide content support for Common Core State Standards (CCSS) in school curricula. An important CCSS goal is for kids to know the difference between primary and secondary sources. With primary sources, the information is firsthand—including information from a witness to an event. A letter written by Lincoln about his Gettysburg Address, for instance. Secondary sources are not from the era described. They are written after the fact, such as an analysis of the Gettysburg Address by a twentieth-century historian.

Use primary sources whenever you can find them. For her three books in Lerner's Our America series, Judith Pinkerton Josephson contacted historical societies for diaries, journals, or letters written by children from other eras. A diary of Kermit Roosevelt, President Teddy Roosevelt's son, detailed childhood pranks like smuggling the family pony up the back steps of the White House to cheer up his sick brother. Judith also incorporated actual songs, games, posters, art, poems, and slogans to give young readers a feel for the times and what children were doing.

Connie Plantz perused old newspaper articles for her biography of Bessie Coleman, the first African American aviatrix, for clues about her personality and determination. For her Elvis Presley biography, Plantz interviewed neighbors, his tailor, and a bodyguard in Memphis, Tennessee.

Spotlight on Biography

 Be a good sleuth. Researching is like unraveling a mystery. Keep asking questions, and don't rely upon other previously published works. Make your words match the era about which you're writing.

—Judith Pinkerton Josephson, *Jesse Owens: Legendary Gold Medal Olympian, Armando and the Blue Tarp School, Nitty-Gritty Grammar,* and more

Fascinated by people who are inventive, daring, caring, wise? Biographies may be your path to children's writing, and, thanks to the Common Core State Standards emphasis on nonfiction, there will be an increased emphasis on the nonfiction market.

TIP

Be a savvy writer. Learn about Common Core and consider providing a Reader's Guide for your work as Randy Morrison has done with his inventive *Seven Moon Circus* (7mc.com), the adventures of a wild boy in a space-traveling circus. Learn how the quagga wangled its way into his lively manuscript.

Biographies anchor readers in different times, provide role models, and inspire. Students meet intriguing people, learn ways to overcome challenges, discover a person's place in history, and gain empathy by walking in another person's shoes.

In some ways writing a biography is like writing a term paper—you do research, credit your sources with footnotes or endnotes, and write a cohesive manuscript. But a strictly encyclopedic manuscript won't sell. Young readers need events woven together into a whole. You must bring your subject to life with anecdotes that highlight important qualities and memorable quirks. Find this person's passion and place in history. Be truthful, accurate, authentic.

Ask yourself what overarching idea you want your readers to take away. That's the key to your subject. Write this idea on a sticky note for your monitor. All your chapters should support that theme. For example, here's my central thesis for my biography on Dr. Barbara McClintock: Through her brilliant research, Barbara McClintock changed the world of genetics.

Quotes are powerful and give insight into a person's personality. Biographer Marie Shepard noted that Maria Montessori, who spoke at the graduation of her class from medical school, said later, "I felt like a lion tamer that day."

Much has changed from the days of the Landmark biographies I grew up on with their invented dialogue and fanciful take on facts. Any words in quotations marks in your biography must be words actually said or written by the person. Invented lines—"Wake up, Wilbur. We test our plane today," said Orville—won't cut it in most of today's biographies. Use primary sources for dialogue: interviews, newspapers, adult biographies, letters.

The one exception could be called biographical narrative history, as in *Alvin Ailey*. Author Andrea Davis Pinkney noted in the back matter that she created constructed dialogue to "weave the story together" for young readers.

Think of a unique approach. Pam Muñoz Ryan based *Amelia and Eleanor Go for a Ride* on a newspaper clipping she came upon about Amelia Earhart taking Eleanor Roosevelt on her first airplane ride. Ryan built this picture book biography around that single incident. In *Martin's Big Words*, Doreen Rappaport used Dr. King's own words to portray his ideals and leadership. Kathleen Krull uses gossip to propel her Lives of . . . series, starting with *Lives of the Musicians: Good Times, Bad times, and What the Neighbors Thought*. (Note the illustrious illustrators for these books: Brian Selznick, Bryan Collier, and Kathryn Hewitt, respectively.)

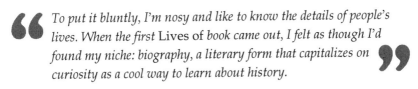

> To put it bluntly, I'm nosy and like to know the details of people's lives. When the first Lives of book came out, I felt as though I'd found my niche: biography, a literary form that capitalizes on curiosity as a cool way to learn about history.

> —Kathleen Krull, *Lives of the Explorers*, the Lives of . . . series, *Wilma Unlimited*, *The Beatles Were Fab (and They Were Funny)*, and more

Once you decide to write a biography, be sure to track all details of your research. Note every resource used, every contact made, including the date, phone numbers, email addresses, websites, book titles, authors, and page numbers. Everyone in my critique group who has done biographies has bemoaned an avoidable research glitch, from footnote hiccups to lost sources.

Also, delight in the search for information. One good lead can send you on the way to another. At the same time, you'll have to curb your enthusiasm. Researching can be so fascinating that you dig and dig. At some point, you must start (and complete!) the writing process. When you do, be smart. Be practical. Evaluate how much you're being paid for the project and how much time it's wise to spend on it. Always write to the grade level of your audience, and use primary sources.

Primary resources are crucial for accuracy. At the American Philosophical Society I had access to photos of geneticist Barbara McClintock and her family, meticulous maize research notes on three-by-five cards, and many of her degrees and award certificates. At the Pinkerton Detective Agency, Judith

Pinkerton Josephson (no relation!) held Allan Pinkerton's codebook in her hand. The Library of Congress also proved valuable in her research.

Speaking of accuracy, for her Jesse Owens biography, Judith consulted four different track and field agencies to find the correct measurement of his gold medal-winning long jump. These sources didn't agree. She finally was able to dig up the correct measurement: 26' 5.5"! Recently, in converting this biography to an ebook, Judith discovered that although other biographers claimed Jesse Owens was the youngest of ten children, he actually had a younger sister named Pearline.

Research can include interviews, adult biographies, diaries and letters, films and documentaries. Information abounds on the Internet, but it's vital to triangulate your data, that is, verify facts by using three solid sources. Whatever you do, don't cram every single research fact you've gleaned into your manuscript. I was so excited about the recognition that came to Barbara McClintock after many decades of meticulous, solitary research that I wrote a whole page about her honors and awards. "Choose the top three," advised my wise editor.

I was gathering fodder for my biography of popular children's writer Gary Paulsen when he spoke to a crowd of devoted readers at the White Rabbit bookstore in La Jolla. As he described a harrowing incident from his second Iditarod run, I was scribbling as fast as my pen would go. Every so often, a sixth grade boy sitting beside me—a huge Paulsen fan—reached over with his pen, grinned, and filled in words I'd missed. (This is why we write for kids.)

Learn more about the process that turned these two biographies into Spotlight Biography ebooks when they went out of print (see page 158).

Fiction

 I really enjoy writing realistic fiction for middle-grade kids. Age 10 to 14 is my sweet spot. What a great way to get young readers to learn about history!

> — Andrea Davis Pinkney, *Raven in a Dove House, Hand in Hand, With the Might of Angels,* and more

Character, Plot, and Setting

Whole books are written on plot, character, setting, voice, tension, point of view, humor, and more. Be patient. Your understanding of these wide-ranging topics will come with time.

Here's a sneak preview on character, setting, and plot. Ease into these three big topics — how you create characters kids will love, engage these characters in the action of your plot, and weave the setting seamlessly into your story.

Character

 When writing for children, you have to respect child development. Children are interested in different things at different ages and books allow them to try on being someone else and have adventures that are not otherwise available to them.

— Janice Yuwiler, co-regional advisor, SCBWI San Diego, *Great Medical Discoveries: Insulin* (Great Medical Discoveries), and more

For many children's writers, characters drive their books. Who will populate your pages? You must know them well. Their hopes, fears, needs, problems, and goals. How they think, their varied backgrounds, their quirks, how they interact, and what they want. These personal traits propel your story and make it compelling.

Make your characters unique. Each one must sound, look, and act in ways different from other characters. If your rejection letter reads, "I just didn't love your characters," they're due for a makeover. Human beings are layered, complex. If your characters are two-dimensional or stereotypical, editors won't buy and readers won't relate.

This means no totally nicey-nice or baddy-bad characters. People have flaws. The folks who populate your books, from picture book to YA, must be three-dimensional. Read *Fiction Is Folks: How to Create Unforgettable Characters*, by Robert Newton Peck, who has written *A Day No Pigs Would Die, Soup, A Part of the Sky*, and other great reads. Note these gripping titles.

Ask your characters questions. Know their appearance. Interview them. Be consistent. All of your characters must be true to themselves. You'll have them learn, grow, and change over the course of your book, but beware of making them do something completely out of character. You'll jolt your readers.

The late Pam Conrad, author of *Prairie Songs* and other titles, gave every character in her books a secret, even if she never revealed it. When she considered how a character would think, act, and react, Conrad had that secret in mind.

To help readers know who's who, give your characters tags. Does he snap his gum? Do her eyebrows lift? Does he crack his knuckles? Does she tap her foot? Are they glued together, the way a kindergarten soccer team moves around the field as one? Is his smile lopsided? Does she limp? Such tags make your characters distinct and help readers picture who's who.

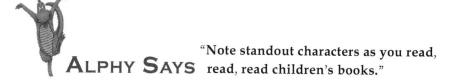

ALPHY SAYS   "Note standout characters as you read, read, read children's books."

Here's a sampling of characters from some of my books:

In *Under the Lemon Moon*, the antagonist is the Night Man, a thief who steals lemons from Rosalinda's tree. But Rosalinda gains insight upon seeing the Night Man sell the lemons to feed his hungry family. And, although the words "forgiveness" and "sharing" never appear, Rosalinda's actions—true to her character—show her ability to forgive and share. Universal qualities.

In *Cryptomania!*, Zander is the "go for it" leader. Stella is the inventor. Cassie, camera in hand, documents the adventures. Theo is the affable "go-along" guy. And Marcus is cautious: "Whoa! Wait! Don't touch that button!" They balance each other as a team. And in the end, it's Marcus's puzzle-solving skills that lead to unraveling the mystery.

In our *Armando and the Blue Tarp School*, Armando is a composite of the real and endearing children Judith Josephson and I met on visits to the school at the Tijuana dump. He longs to learn on the blue tarp at Señor David's school, but his role working in the garbage dump alongside his father is vital to his family. In the end, both Papá and Armando bend a little. We didn't have to invent Señor David, the teacher—he's factually based on David Lynch, the real teacher, now in his third decade of providing education for the poorest of the poor in Tijuana and Matagalpa, Nicaragua.

The kids at Pepper Lane Elementary in *Water, Weed, and Wait* nicknamed Mr. Barkley "Mr. Barks-a-Lot" for his grumpiness at playground noise and kickballs that fly into his backyard. But when timid Ben peeks through a knothole in the fence, he discovers the neighbor's secret—a lush garden. Ben summons his courage and tells Mr. Barkley about the plans for a school garden. Mr. B. joins the project, albeit gruffly at first. As the kids get to know him, he softens, providing a big, funny finish at the celebratory garden party.

The cricket in *Cricket at the Manger* is also a grump. His wing is injured, so his song begins as "GAR-UMPH! GAR-RICKET!" Readers may know the Nativity story, but still be intrigued to find a new character and discover what makes his tune change to "CHIRRR-RUP, CHIRRR-RICKET!"

> 1. *Characters are like children. Who you want them to be is irrelevant. It's who they want to be that's important.*
>
> 2. *Don't try to be a good writer; try to be an honest one.*
>
> 3. *Write to ask questions, not to find answers.*

—Michael Mahin, *Muddy: The Story of Muddy Waters* and *Stalebread Charlie and the Razzy Dazzy Spasm Band* (both 2017, www.michaelmahin.com)

Plot

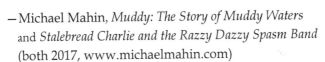

ALPHY SAYS   **"We're talking fiction here, but some of this can apply to nonfiction, too."**

You've started working on your characters. Now for plot.

When you check out a book's back cover or book jacket, you want to know what the book's about. That's the plot teaser. Plot is the structure of your story. Your road map. For writers, it's the "What if . . .?" that drives the story.

From picture book to new adult, much goes into plot: hook, conflict, rising action, climax, falling action, and powerful ending. Layer your plot with convincing characters, strong action, and vivid settings so the whole shebang resonates and satisfies your readers.

A fiction book has conflict at its core: problems or obstacles for your character to overcome. Questions are the key to holding your reader's interest. What happens next? What does your main character want? What obstacles are in the way? How are these roadblocks handled?

 Make sure on every page, everyone wants something, even if it's a glass of water.

—Kurt Vonnegut, *Slaughterhouse-Five, Cat's Cradle,* and more

Pam Conrad also knew the importance of upping the ante. In *Prairie Songs,* we watch a sophisticated, educated New York lady standing in her fashionable gown in unknown territory—the prairie. In one of her first actions, she dons gloves to gather the dried cow plops to use for fuel. Readers immediately ask themselves, "Can this fragile, proper city-dweller survive in an environment so alien to her?"

When plotting, put your characters in peril. The line "Chase your character up a tree and throw rocks at him or her" is all over the Internet. Would that we could credit the wise sage who concocted this visual!

Beginnings are critical. They're the "hook"—you must snag your readers from the get-go. Richard Peck advises you to ask, "Is there a question?" The first line of his *The Mouse with the Question Mark Tail* reads, "Every time a human walks out of a room, something with more feet walks in." E. B. White's *Charlotte's Web,* that timeless classic, begins, "Where's Papa going with that axe?" Right away, trouble is brewing. (Look out, Wilbur!)

My first draft of *Under the Lemon Moon* had Rosalinda asleep in her bed in her Mexican village, moonlight shining in on her eyelashes, blah blah blah. All grammatically and syntactically correct but, ugh. Nothing grabby. The first line now reads, "Deep in the night, Rosalinda heard noises."

With this tight, rhythmic opener, kids can't help but read on, questions swirling in their heads: What's going on? What's making those noises? What will Rosalinda do? With each of these openers, "who, what, where, why" questions flow in. That's exactly what you want in your opener.

In Your Journal

Start a list of first lines from the children's books you're scouring. I still have a birthday present I made my mom: a blank journal dubbed *Book Sandwiches*. In it I wrote out the powerful first and last lines of books we both loved. From Nevil Shute to Rumer Godden, Josephine Tey to L. Frank Baum (we devoured all the Oz books), those openers and endings could trigger for us the delicious scenes we'd enjoyed between those openings and endings. What joy lies between the covers of books.

Endings are as important as beginnings. You want your readers to feel that satisfied "ahhhh" at the end. Almost all children's book end with hope or at least strike a positive note. And both editors and readers love a clever twist. Note that adults can't rush to the rescue. The young characters who populate your book must solve the dilemma themselves.

Two words for you: Plot Whisperer! If the name Martha Alderson (marthaalderson.com) hasn't crossed your radar, let it be a big blip now. The Plot Whisperer will help guide you to the heart of your story.

Setting

Whether you plop your characters into ancient Greece, the Big Apple, or outer space, a strong setting will ground your readers and make your story believable. Including the five senses helps you achieve realism no matter what your setting.

Do readers hear the *clop-clop* of horses' hooves on cobblestone or the *whish* of a theme park monorail? Is that venison so far gone it makes your starving character gag? Is the edge of the manor door splintered? Does the thief's flashlight glint off the gold-leafed museum frame? Has a thunderstorm washed the air so clean that your character, fleeing his enemy, stops to breathe in the scent?

IN YOUR JOURNAL

Do this prewrite to nail a setting using the five senses.

Label five columns sight, sound, scent, taste, and touch. Choose a location — the attic, a hockey stadium, the planet Panquor, the tundra, a Wisconsin lake, an earring store, Gettysburg, a schoolroom in ancient China, a tsunami-ravaged shore, or a location in your own manuscript — then set a timer for five minutes. Pour words and ideas into each column. What do you see there? Hear? Smell?

Taste? Feel? Jot quickly — you'll have great fodder for scene building.

Since I've not yet published MG or YA, I turned to my friend Deborah Halverson for insights into how setting can affect characters in these books. She's been a book editor and is now an award-winning author of *Writing Young Adult Fiction for Dummies* and *Writing New Adult Fiction*. She's written YA books and provides freelance editing. She's on the advisory board for UC San Diego Extension's Children's Book Writing and Children's Book Illustration certificate programs and she's the one who compiles the annual marketing report for SCBWI. She also answers writers' questions at her Dear Editor bog (deareditor.com). So listen up. In the section below, Deborah suggests rethinking how *where* you put your people helps you craft rich MG/YA characters.

Deborah Halverson, on setting and character:

Too often in their efforts to hold young readers' interest, writers of middle grade and young adult fiction rely on plot events, physical description, and dialogue to develop their characters, missing out on another powerful characterization tool: setting. You can enhance your characterization by showing the characters acting upon or reacting to their setting's props and environmental elements. Here are three ways to do that:

> **Put characters in places that push them.** Don't always pick familiar, expected places for your scenes, such as a kid's bedroom or the lunch court. Pick places that can reveal your character's personality, mood, state of mind, concerns, or physical abilities or limitations in fresh ways, and that will push the character out of

his comfort zone and thus push your story forward. Consider a kid rebelling against his parents and their rules. Instead of having the kid confront Mom and Dad in the familiar living room with lots of arguing to reveal their moods and conflict, you could send the family to Parent Night at school, where they must do the punch-and-cookies chatty thing and where the parent/teacher commiserating would send the family's emotional tension through the roof. Instead of cliché arguing, you'd get verbal jousting and painful subtext that's as refreshing as it is revealing. A shy or antisocial kid would chafe at this event even without the simmering rebellion.

Show your characters reacting to the elements. A character who's unhappy at his after-school job might complain about his duties and fight with his coworkers — that's action, dialogue, and conflict, all of which are good. But you can go a step further and make the setting a big part of his work scenes, emphasizing his displeasure. How about if we move his job outdoors and have him reacting to the scorching sun, sweating in his pits and refusing to fully raise his arms around his coworkers? Imagine him rolling a dewy soda can on his forehead while the sun beats on his neck and he dreams about jobs he'd rather have. He could be startled when passing cars honk, then step in dog poop, dodge sprinklers that pop on unexpectedly, and, reaching the breaking point, turn and flip the bird at yet another honking motorist — only to discover he's just flipped off the girl he's been crushing on. His reactions to the setting elements reveal his wishes and set him up for a mistake that will push the story forward. All the while, the fictional world deepens as we experience the sensations of that environment along with the character.

Make your characters interact with the props. Let's return to that doggie doo on the sidewalk, if you can stand it. That prop is particular to that setting. Put props in your settings that are distinct to that place, then have your character interact with them. A kid who squeezes into a straight-backed dining room chair at Nana's hand-carved table reveals a different personality or concern than a kid who drags that chair away from Nana's table, screeching its legs on the hardwood floor, then spins the neighboring chair sideways so he can kick up his feet and practically lie across the two chairs. Disrespectful much, fella?

A story full of small setting-related moments becomes a rich collection of character revelation. Combine this with your other tools—description, dialogue, and action—to sculpt rich characters who feel "real" to your young readers.

Thanks, Deborah, from all of us.
(Visit Deborah's website, www.deborahhalverson.com.)

Diversity and Multiculturalism

> 66 *Take stock of the diversity of your characters. Is everyone in your story white and straight and upper middle class and thin and good looking and third-generation American? That's not the world kids and teens today live in. Books are a mirror and a window. Give every kid a chance to see themselves reflected in the characters you create. And let them see their shared humanity with those who, on the surface, may seem so different from themselves, but aren't so different after all.* 99

— Lee Wind, award-winning blogger

The importance of diversity in children's books has been much in the news lately. Kids need books where they see themselves reflected on the page. Publishers are responding.

At LinkedIn's SCBWI blog, Chelsea Mooser Confalone notes that since the nonprofit First Book—with its huge purchasing power—has stepped in with the promise to buy more diverse books, "they will be able to get publishing houses to buy and publish more diverse manuscripts from new and existing authors."

Know the publishers that already support diversity. Lee & Low Books (www.leeandlow.com) is a great example. This well-established, award-winning, independent publisher specializes in multicultural books. Young readers will see themselves reflected on the covers and the pages of their books. Their Tu Books imprint focuses on fantasy, science fiction, and mystery featuring people of color in worlds inspired by non-Western folklore or culture. Their newly acquired Shen's Books imprint introduces readers to the culture of Asia.

Whether you're new to GLBT (gay, lesbian, bisexual, transgender) issues (
already on board, recognize that a percentage of all our young readers are
gay. These kids both need and deserve the insight, empathy, and support of
writers like you. Like any underserved group, they need to find themselves in
the words and illustrations of books they read.

The 2014 California School Library Association conference included the workshop
"LGBTQ Panel: Making Diversity Work in School Libraries." Moderator Lee
Wind and fellow panelists Eric Shanower (award-winning illustrator and the
Oz expert in our San Diego SCBWI chapter, ericshanower.com), Chris Enterline,
and Tommy Kovac provided valuable insights, resources, and humor.

All four stressed the need for allies who will speak up for these young people.
(For information on books, organization, and materials that Lee posted after
the conference, Google the panel title.)

Artist Tommy Kovac, who calls himself "a library guy," noted, "If you're
working in a library and the atmosphere makes you nervous or afraid to
display and promote diversity, then your library desperately needs it."

Explore the We need Diverse Books campaign (weneeddiversebooks.org),
and on Tumblr, Twitter, and Facebook to discover more about their goals,
programs, resources, and awards.

CHAPTER 3

The Road to Strong Writing

Your Singular Writing Path

Your writing road won't match anyone else's. What worked for me may not work for you. I taught for years—elementary, middle school, college extension. I eased into writing with articles, stories, columns. Then I turned to writing books for kids. Some of you will leapfrog over baby steps like these and dive immediately into the challenges of getting a book published.

Your path is yours alone. Unique. Go to your strengths.

 Writing is easy. All you have to do is cross out the wrong words.

> —Mark Twain (1835–1910), *Adventures of Tom Sawyer,*
> *Adventures of Huckleberry Finn,* and more

I read widely. But I know deep inside that I am not going to produce compelling science fantasy or teen mystery. These could, however, be your strengths.

In Your Journal

Assess your interests and strengths. Consider which children's books you're reading.

Write your responses to questions like these:

- What children's book genre pulls me?
- As I dive into the picture book world, what books do I choose?
- Do I lean toward fiction or nonfiction in my adult reading?
- At conferences, which sessions do I attend?

Keep building your knowledge base. Mark one day a month from now on your calendar for reading over the list you just created and adding to this personal list.

 It doesn't matter if you've gone to some fancy writing school. It doesn't matter if you've got a byline or your name on a book. You don't even have to be paid for your writing. You are a writer because you write. Writing comes from within. Being a writer is as much a part of who you are as what you do. Answer this: If you had all the money in the world to do anything you please, *would you still write?*

—Wendy Kitts, *Sable Island: The Wandering Sandbar*
(www.wendykitts.ca)

Something Will Be Hard

Everyone has writing strengths. Some of you are great at writing to tight outlines. Some can create mouth-watering, rhythmic sentences that beg to be read aloud. Maybe you love making appearances and marketing or relish the solitude that lets you create new worlds.

But no writer finds every aspect of writing a finger snap. Will fashioning a believable setting be your sticking point? Perhaps plot. Or suspense. You may shiver just thinking about sending out your work. Social media may strike you as a time sponge. Rejection may hit you hard and make you consider giving it all up. The idea of marketing could appall you.

Shadows of doubt can fall on this writing enterprise of yours when:

- You're stuck.
- You've had three rejections in a row.
- The "big" children's writers win yet another award.
- You see the scale, breadth, and depth of the field.
- You see the scale, breadth, and depth of *your* project.
- Your personal life overwhelms your writing life.

Life's like that—some things are easy. Others are hard. When you are discouraged, you have two choices: quit or carry on. It's up to you.

To become a children's writer, there's only one thing to do. Keep on keeping on. Baby steps. Baby steps.

Be Still

My mom used the world's first textspeak. "FMIEM," she'd laugh: "First mistake I ever made." What I heard was, "Mistakes happen. Get over it and move on."

She'd write "QDAH" on her calendar for Quiet Day at Home. These days, since we more often view the tops of people's heads than their faces because their noses are in their electronic devices, it's clear that we need time unplugged. This is especially true of people who write.

At the 2012 SCBWI conference, keynoter Deborah Underwood spoke of the need for quiet in the creative process: "We don't owe it to ourselves to make time for quiet; we owe it to the kids who will read our books."

Your brain is writing even when you're not at your computer. You may think you'll remember the ingenious flashes that come to you as you drift to sleep, but keeping a notebook or tablet/smart phone at your bedside guarantees they won't turn to vapor at dawn's early light.

Renowned author Karen Cushman says she's writing even while deadheading roses. At the outdoor pool near our house I've practiced speeches, figured out plots, named characters, and had titles pop into my head while jogging in the shallow end or doing laps. Thus the importance of my waterproof space pen and a piece of cardboard from a Cheerios box stashed at the pool's edge. I may be dripping wet but I don't lose the ideas.

In a TED Talk, Carl Honoré suggested you "get in touch with your inner tortoise." Find quiet. Turn off the phone, radio, TV, tech devices. Stay off your email. Let your family cope without you. Breathe and think and wonder. Your writing will be stronger for it.

In Your Journal

Where do you find quiet? Write about that place or places for three minutes. What draws you there? What do you gain? How to you feel?

TIP

Need a laugh? Check out the annual Bulwer-Lytton Fiction Contest (www.bulwer-lytton.com) where "WWW" means "Wretched Writers Welcome." Get a hoot from these appalling first sentences, then deliberately pen your own. Share with your critique group.

Traps, Tricks, Treachery

Remember Steve Irwin, TV's animal adventurer who'd say, "Dayn-jah, dayn-jah, dayn-jah" in his brash Aussie accent?

There's danger in some writing waters . . .

Getting Input From Loved Ones

Don't. Their "I just love your story" is utterly unhelpful. If you do share your work, you want people who know writing and will offer truly helpful suggestions, not chirpy kudos that don't make your work stronger.

Talking Heads

If your picture book characters spend all their time talking to each other, you give the illustrator nothing but "talking heads" to draw. Where's the action? What's the predicament? Where are the set changes?

Message Books

Don't set yourself up for rejection. If your goal is to teach kids a lesson, you're in the wrong business. You're not Aesop. No, "The moral of the story is . . ." No, "That's how the little bunny learned that it's not nice to . . ."

Linear Plots

This happened, then this, then this, and then—wow—this happened. Your real life may take you from work to the grocery to the dentist's and home, but a string of incidents like those does not cut it. Engage your readers and your characters in meaningful action. There's no tension, nothing to resolve if you just string together a series of events.

Sagging Middles (or Beginnings or Endings)

Read your work closely. Aloud. If your mind drifts, cut. Or raise the tension. Or introduce an intriguing subplot. Here's Stephen King on pacing: "Mostly when I think of pacing, I go back to Elmore Leonard, who explained it so perfectly by saying he just left out the boring parts."

Using Every Speck of Research

I know. You've done all this background work. You've found numerous sources. Done heaps of research. It's all information you needed to know. But your reader doesn't. As mentioned earlier in the biography section, avoid piling every detail into your manuscript. Be choosy. Ask, "What will paint the scene or add dash to this person without making my readers snore?"

Rhyming Text

Do you equate "picture books" with rhymed verse? Know that hundreds of wincingly bad rhymed manuscripts with forced rhyme and forced rhythm flow weekly into publishers' burgeoning slush piles.

FAQ _____

You: What's a slush pile?

Me: The terms "over the transom" and "slush pile" both refer to unsolicited, unagented work sent to publishing houses.

Rhyming is hard. It's intriguing. If you choose this specialized subgenre, your manuscript must be smooth as a kitten's fur. This means no extra words stuck in to make a line scan. And no inverted syntax: "Thus from the dragon he did flee."

Done right, creating a rhyming manuscript that's a gem is worth every moment curled up with your mighty *Synonym Finder* and rhyming dictionary. Make your poetic work so stellar that readers won't have a clue as to all the painstaking work you put into making the text look and sound effortless.

Read books by Ann Whitford Paul who has taught writing through UCLA Extension. Ann is a picture book author and poet who really knows her iambic pentameter. But somewhere in every manuscript, she adds a surprising element—a close rhyme, or a jog in the rhythm to keep her poetic voice fresh.

TIP

You'll hear that rhyming books are hard to write. (They are.)

And hard to sell. (Also true.)

If you're drawn to poetic writing, go ahead and give it a try. Rhyming books can sell. (Witness my *Cricket at the Manger* and *Sleepytime Me.*)

Seven Deadly Writing Sins

1. Long-winded openers
2. Stereotypical characters
3. Boring passages
4. Jarring grammatical and style errors
5. Pedantic writing
6. Moralizing
7. Unsatisfying endings

Capture Your Ideas

FAQ _____

Kids: Where do you get your ideas?
Me: For most writers, *getting* ideas isn't the problem. *Keeping* them can be.

Put out a BOLO (Be On the Lookout) for fresh ideas. Following trends is pointless. No wizard schools. No vampires. No series of unfortunate events. No demigods. No pigeons driving the bus. Those ships have sailed. You're looking for that wonderfully creative idea that will make an editor sit up and say, "Wowzah! Yes!" (Consider Death as the narrator in Markus Zusak's *The Book Thief*.)

Ideas are all around. They arise from memories, daily life, dreams, your reading, the news, family, trips you take, overheard snippets, classes, personal experiences, and plain old brainstorms. Don't lose these ideas.

James Cross Giblin, an editor and author of eighteen books for young people, knows both sides of the business. I met him at a Highlights Chautauqua conference in the early nineties and still remember one of his vivid anecdotes. Stuck on a plane that was delayed for takeoff, he was seated next to a guy with long hair and a big case. Giblin assumed "rock musician" and strained to think of what they might have in common. As it turned out the fellow was a chimney sweep and the result was, of course, a book about chimney sweeps. (Check out *The Giblin Guide to Writing Children's Books*.)

You never know when an idea will hit—while carpooling, in a business meeting, unclogging the toilet, folding clothes, or sitting at the dentist's office. At a baseball game, grocery store, Laundromat, Eiffel Tower, Thai restaurant, or family gathering. Eating cake at your niece's graduation party? Grab a festive napkin, date it, and capture that flash of inspiration.

This week, start an idea file. It can be simple (one file folder) or complex—sorted into sections for plots, settings, names, historical incidents, how-to, and other subtopics of interest to you. Date each entry and plunk those ideas into your idea file.

Fred Rogers of *Mister Rogers' Neighborhood* suggested that his young viewers think of three things and combine them to tell a story. How about a hippo, a trampoline, and a peppermint ice cream cone. (See? Your brain's working already.) Do the same with your idea file when you're feeling stuck. Pull out three tidbits that could be intriguing when combined.

ALPHY SAYS   **"Your idea file only works if you use it."**

Creativity can't be nailed down. You're tucking away ideas because you never know what will happen when you grab that gem and begin working.

The prolific Eve Bunting reads the *Los Angeles Times* every day and many of her books start with a story plucked from the news. Think *Ducky*, about the shipment of rubber ducks that fell from a cargo ship and floated around the oceans, or her YA novel about teens jumping from a train trestle into the ocean in Carlsbad, California.

Bette Bao Lord combined a sports figure with the Chinese New Year to create the memorable *In the Year of the Boar and Jackie Robinson*. Gennifer Choldenko used the island of Alcatraz for her clever and endearing *Al Capone Does My Shirts*.

Karen Mueller Coombs noted the rise of cell phone sexting among teens and researched the phenomenon — the growing awareness among educators and parents, its repercussions (some minor, some tragic), and the response of law enforcement and the courts. The result is her YA ebook *Finn's Mystery Girl*, told in the voices of two high school guys who inadvertently dig themselves into deeper and deeper trouble after one receives a suggestive photo.

Chance Discoveries and Your Inner Geek

Why do I still love printed books? It's more than the feel of the covers, more than fingering the pages and knowing that I can go back to a phrase I remember seeing (it was on the left side three-quarters of the way down), more than picking up new words and making notes in the margins. It's the discoveries that I make as a reader while on the way to somewhere else.

We're writers. We're curious about everything.

Tap into your curiosity — the word from a book you're reading; an overheard anecdote; a snarky snippet from NPR's *Wait Wait . . . Don't Tell Me!*; a comment on a blog; anything that makes you stop and gives you the *aha!* that winkles its way into your mind.

Capture these fleeting thoughts, these moments of wonder in your journal or idea file. You never know where they'll lead. The prolific genius Kate DiCamillo always has a journal with her and journals in the morning and in the afternoon.

Something from a movie may tweak your interest. As a bibliophile, did you wonder about the books Suzy Bishop read in the film *Moonrise Kingdom*? I did. Turns out they are figments of the scriptwriter's imagination. You can read about these books from the charming, gnomelike narrator of the film, actor Bob Balaban. Google "The Books of Moonrise Kingdom" (www.finebooksmagazine.com).

CHAPTER 4

Picture Book Basics

Because so many new writers ache to write a picture book, I'm giving this genre its own section—the true (realistic) scoop.

If you're serious about pursuing picture books, a great place to start is Ann Whitford Paul's *Writing Picture Books: A Hands-On Guide from Story Creation to Publication.*

 What I love about writing picture books is that they feel like pearls, small, perfectly shaped and shining with rhythm. I love spending time making sure each word expresses not only the story, but the emotion behind it. Even more, I love imagining adults and children, sitting skin to skin, sharing my words. My hope is that those children will like my book enough to want to hear more books and then learn to read their own books. What would a society be without a reading population! The responsibility we bear to start children onto that path is *humbling, terrifying, and exciting.*

—Ann Whitford Paul, *'Twas the Late Night of Christmas*; *Mañana, Iguana*; and more

Good News and Bad News

 ### The Bad News
Many people think they can write a picture book.

More Bad News

More than eighty percent of all manuscripts submitted are for picture books.

Some Good News

As you digest this eighty percent fact, does your brain go on high alert? Does an inner voice say, "Perhaps I'll tackle (fill in the blank: a magazine article or story, nonfiction, a chapter book, a graphic novel) and *then* have a go at a picture book"? Accumulating writing credits to send with your first picture book manuscript adds to your credibility.

More Good News

Unique, compelling, richly-imagined, clever, high-quality, blooper-free picture book manuscripts float to the top.

The Inside Story

In picture books, every word counts. There's no room for meandering. Read your manuscript aloud. Pare and focus your piece.

Today most picture books have 1,000 or fewer words. (Think 500 or fewer). You don't have the luxury of extraneous thoughts. Every single word must carry its own weight. Mem Fox's *Tough Boris* has 78 words. My *Sleepytime Me* has 132.

Think three: three pigs, three wishes, three billy goats gruff. Goldilocks tastes three bowls of porridge, tries three chairs, tests three beds. Think three, too, with plot bumps, each more serious than the last.

As with any writing, your opener is critical. Grab your young readers by their jammies and pull them in.

Picture books must withstand the test of time. Beloved books are read aloud again and again by patient parents, babysitters, relatives, and teachers. They must be solid and endearing, not a one-shot read.

Many picture books are light, funny, joyful, rollicking. Others are quieter, like Jane Yolen's *Owl Moon*, a Caldecott Medal winner. Picture books also tackle tough topics. Patricia MacLachlan and illustrator Steven Kellogg used their combined decades of experience to create *Snowflakes Fall* after the tragedy at Sandy Hook Elementary School. For children experiencing a grandparent with Alzheimer's disease or other form of dementia, Mem Fox wrote *Wilfrid Gordon McDonald Partridge*. Patricia Polacco's *Pink and Say* features two friends in Civil War times, one black, one white. Explore books like these, where art and words combine to touch the heart. You may be just the person to write such a book.

TIP

Encourage active listening. In Isaac Olaleye's *Bitter Bananas* (illustrated by Ed Young), the words "Oh yes, oh yes!" and "Oh no, oh no!" echo through the text. In Pam Muñoz Ryan's *Mice and Beans*, Abuela sets a mousetrap each night to this rhythmic refrain: "When it was set and ready to snap she turned out the lights and went to bed." Kids love to chant repeats like these and become part of the storytelling.

Text and Format

 A picture book writer must foster the craft of telling a good story while cleverly leaving space for the illustrator. Pick up a published picture book and transcribe its text into a separate document. By stripping away the illustrations you'll see exactly what the author wrote, and just as important, what he or she didn't write.

— Brooke Bessesen, founder and director of Authors for Earth Day, *Zachary Z. Packrat Backpacks the Grand Canyon*, *Look Who Lives in the Ocean!*, and more (www.brookebessesen.com; www.authorsforearthday.org)

The standard length for picture books is 32 pages. (Some books for younger readers are 16 pages, and some, like my *Cryptomania!*, run 48 pages, but these are exceptions.) Visit Picturing Books (www.picturingbooks.com) to learn about parts of a picture book.

To get a sense of whether your picture book is working, make a dummy. That's a 32-page mock-up. Fold paper to create 32 pages. Number them. Even numbers are on the left; odd on the right. Skip four or five pages to allow for copyright page, dedication, and title page. Picture books most often start on the right, on page 5. But if the illustrator opens with a full-page spread (one illustration that covers both pages), it will cover pages 4 and 5. Your great wrap-up, the punch, the twist, the "awww" moment—most often lands on page 32, the final page turn. If your book has back matter—additional information about your topic—your ending may come sooner. *Armando* and *Water, Weed, and Wait* both include back matter, helpful in classrooms as teachers follow Common Core Standards to work with their darlings on close reading.

Print your picture book text, then cut and paste it into your dummy to see how the words might fit on 27 or 28 pages. You'll discover a lot when you evaluate your manuscript in the form of the actual pages of a book:

- Do the page turns work?
- Too long? Too short to cover 27 pages? (This is rare.)
- Enough variety in your settings?
- Talking heads? (Lots of dialogue; little opportunity for an illustrator to soar.)
- Are page breaks balanced or are there too many words here, not enough there?
- Limp characters?
- Boring parts you can chop?
- Are plot points well timed?
- Lack of action?
- Emotional pull?
- Laughs?

Before submitting a picture book, I sometimes put double spaces in the manuscript to show potential page turns. Save such a doc for your own use. You don't need to include double breaks on the manuscript you send. Decisions on page turns lie ultimately with your editor, the graphic designer, and the illustrator, but it's fun to see how close you come.

Illustrations: The Big Picture

Remember this FAQ from the start of this book?

FAQ _____

You: How do I find an illustrator for my picture book?
Me: You don't.

True confession. The first story I wrote was about a boy named Jeremy Potter. (This was pre-Harry.) I naively gave what I thought was a clever manuscript to a talented artist friend to illustrate. She misread "Potter" and made the main character an otter. A sweet otter, but an otter.

I'd goofed in so many ways. First, the piece wasn't strong enough to be a book. It was my first go at a picture book and I wasn't ready, hadn't done my research, hadn't *practiced* writing, hadn't put in the time, hadn't read enough current picture books. Second, and this is bold for a reason, **you don't find the illustrator.**

If you're brand new, here's the startling news: Publishers have their own stables of artists whose unique styles, credits, professionalism, and reliability are known. The publishers are the Match.com for your work. They seek out the perfect illustration partner for your work — one with a striking style who can create pages with art to pull readers in. Trust your editor and the graphic designer to make the match.

You may be further surprised to learn that the writer and illustrator rarely communicate prior to publication. The publishing house handles two major jobs:

1. Words — giving the editorial support to make your book strong as it can be.
2. Illustrations — working with the artist they choose to bring your words to life.

After publication (not before), you and the illustrator can communicate directly and work together on marketing.

Thinking of submitting a manuscript with your own art? Here's one word for you: wonderstruck. That's both the title of Brian Selznick's remarkable book, *Wonderstruck*, and also how an editor must feel in looking at a piece you both write and illustrate. It can be done. Think Jan Brett, Richard Jesse Watson, Patricia Polacco, Steven Kellogg, Eric Carle, and others. But unless you're one of the lucky, super-talented few who stars at both writing and illustrating, stick with writing. Leave the illustrator choice to your publisher.

You can handicap your submissions by including art — your own or a friend's. Your friend may be a talented artist, but here's the rub: Editors get cranky when art accompanies manuscripts. They may love the art, but not the story. Or love the story, but not the art. If you still want to send both manuscript and art, be sure to state clearly that you'll be happy for the editor to consider both separately. Sending both as a unit (with a "take the whole thing or leave it" attitude) is a big risk and substantially lowers your chance of acceptance.

Drilling Down: Illustration Specifics

Most picture books are done by teams, put together by the editor of an established publishing house. One person writes; the other draws. These two work independently. The best books happen this way. Illustrators don't want (or need!) an author looking over their shoulders as they draw. And vice-versa. Think of editors as the cool-headed mediators and midwives. They will look to what's best for the book itself.

> —Joy Chu, art director/designer, with 30+ years experience in the publishing industry; advisor, UCSD Extension Children's Book Illustration & Writing Certificate Programs; instructor, children's book illustration, UCSD Extension

Tempted to add notes to the illustrator? Perhaps something like this: "Here's what my characters look like. Here's the setting. On page three Howie is jumping from the garage roof in his supercape flying, clinging to a big golf umbrella."

Don't. Don't, don't, don't. Illustrators are brilliant visual thinkers. They get free rein. Trust them. And make a sweep through your picture book manuscript to look specifically for descriptions you've included that can be dumped because they'll show in the pictures. You'll further shorten your text and further tilt the wheel of acceptance your way.

Exception: If you use the word "pipers," you could be thinking of bagpipes or birds. Add a short note, flush right:

[Art note: sandpipers]

When people ask who illustrates my books, I just smile. I've never had the same artist twice. My different publishers have chosen wisely, matching the feel and styles of my manuscripts to the perfect illustrator.

Artists add so much to picture books. You and your illustrator are partners. And that's why picture book advances and royalties are split between writer and illustrator. Since you need to be savvy about the whole picture book, not just the words, here's the inside story of my picture books.

Sleepytime Me

(Random House Books for Young Readers)

In *Sleepytime Me*, artist Christopher Denise, whom my editor dubbed "a genius with light," created luminous illustrations, adding depth and continuity to this bedtime story for sleepyheads in ways I couldn't have dreamed of.

Under the Lemon Moon

(Lee & Low Books)

Illustrator René King Moreno chose soft hues to depict the Mexican countryside. To heighten the magical realism of my text, Moreno added outsize butterflies and dragonflies throughout the book. She also gave Rosalinda a baby brother, rounding out the family. When I asked Liz Szabla, my editor, if we should name this sweet boy and give him a couple of speaking lines, she said, "No. He's making a cameo appearance."

Cryptomania!: Teleporting into Greek and Latin with the CryptoKids

(Park Dale Media; originally Tricycle Press)

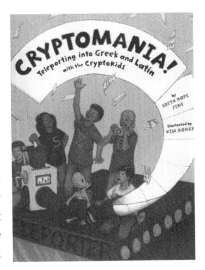

Illustrator Kim Doner digs Greek and Latin roots. She caught on fast to the Teleporter and its travels. She used completely different art styles for the eight different Teleporter destinations—a classical look for Ancient Greece and Rome, a cartoony Flintstone look for the Alphasaurus Academy, and so on. We'd never met, but Kim visited my website and included a yellow moon on the opening Building Blocks pages, a surprise tip of the hat to my *Under the Lemon Moon*. Look for her details—plastic wrap windows for the refrigerator-box Teleporter, bread and peanut butter for the hungry travelers, a cleverly rendered clue the CryptoKids misunderstand, and mysterious green letters that appear in the photos Cassie takes along the way.

Armando and the Blue Tarp School

(Lee & Low Books, with Judith Pinkerton Josephson)

By outlining houses, people, and objects in white, illustrator Hernán Sosa created a look that mimics stained glass. The white line you see is the original surface, the paper he began with. We still can't imagine this painstaking, detailed work, but this technique, while portraying the truth of what it was like for Armando and his family to live and work at the Tijuana dump, also softens the images, making them palatable for young readers. Young artists get their noses close to the pages to study Sosa's illustrations.

Water, Weed, and Wait

(Tricycle Press, with Angela Demos Halpin)

Illustrator Colleen M. Madden chose a palette like Italian gelato. Her whimsical style appeals to both students and adults—librarians, teachers, master gardeners—who read this book aloud to kiddos. She captured Miss Marigold, our garden lady, perfectly. And grumpy neighbor Mr. Barkley grows friendlier through the pages. We love the 3-D effect of the double-page spread with the ladybugs: they're small in the background and large in the foreground, as if flying right up to the kids who read the book.

Cricket at the Manger

(Boyds Mills Press)

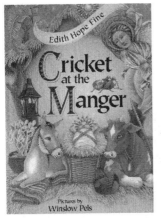

In *Cricket*, illustrator Winslow Pels created collage magic using actual pieces of jewelry for stars and glinting bits in the wool of the lambs' fleece. The backdrop for each illustration is—I kid you not—sandpaper. (This I discovered when I asked my editor where they'd found such beautiful textured paper for the book.) She chose a medieval-style cricket, added the best cow ever, and designed elegant woodcut letters to start the text on each page.

Bonus Tips

Holiday Books

Everyone seems to think holiday books are easy to write, but books about popular holidays are a hard sell. For a publisher to express interest, your holiday book must stand far above the crowded field.

Christmas is second only to Halloween in manuscript topics received by publishers. You're also up against the likes of Chris Van Allsburg's *The Polar Express* and a picture book adaptation of Charles Dickens' *A Christmas Carol*. Above all, don't write about your own child riding with Santa on Christmas Eve. Editors have seen that idea hundreds of times.

Think smart. Consider spotlighting lesser-known holidays. If you're determined to write a Halloween or Christmas book, do it when you've published other books, have strong reviews (some awards don't hurt), good sales figures, and a social media presence.

Team Up!

Great ideas for strengthening your picture book skills can hatch in your local SCBWI. Here in San Diego, Andrea Zimmerman had the brainstorm to start Picture Book Party, a monthly gathering held over the course of two years for published members specifically interested in picture books. Everyone brought published picture books to share that focused on a specific topic. As a reminder to be daring about our own submissions, Andrea passed a bike horn. We honked the horn for every manuscript we had out circulating. Andrea made us laugh and encouraged us with positive reinforcement. Visit her *Picture Book Party* blog (www.picturebookparty.com). The subtitle says it all — *Picture Book Party: Creating and Celebrating Picture Books*!

Finally, heed these words from the late Charlotte Zolotow, author and editor:

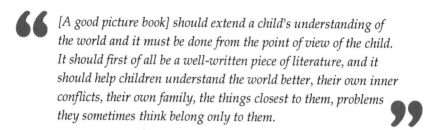

> *[A good picture book] should extend a child's understanding of the world and it must be done from the point of view of the child. It should first of all be a well-written piece of literature, and it should help children understand the world better, their own inner conflicts, their own family, the things closest to them, problems they sometimes think belong only to them.*

—Charlotte Zolotow (1915–2013), *This Quiet Lady, Over and Over, Some Things Go Together, William's Doll*, and more

TIP

These days, zeroing in on a specific topic like writing picture books is easy to do online. Just be sure to evaluate the site for veracity. (They want money? Exit!)

CHAPTER 5

Rock Your Grammar

Grammar is a key writing tool. To achieve your goal of publication, make correct grammar a no-brainer.

 You'll want grammar on the top shelf of your toolbox and don't annoy me with your moans of exasperation and your cries that you don't understand grammar. You never DID understand grammar. And you flunked that whole semester in sophomore English.

—Stephen King, *On Writing: A Memoir of the Craft*

Blunt. True.

Feeling rusty? Here's a quick review. (Ready? Cue the froggy's hand for Thumbs Up and Thumbs Down!)

Pesky Pronouns

Between you and **me** (not **I**!), I see and hear pronoun errors daily. Such errors are red flags for editors.

Pronouns as Subjects

The pronouns *I, he, she, we,* and *they* are **subject**ive pronouns, used as **subjects**.

What is wrong with this party planning?

"Ask Jennifer. Her and me are in charge of the cake."
"Me and Alex are headed to Costco."
"Check with Jorge. Trevor and him will do clean-up and recycling."

"Ask Jennifer. She and I are in charge of the cake."
"Alex and I are headed to Costco."
"Check with Jorge. Trevor and he will do clean-up and recycling."

Pronouns as Objects

The pronouns *me, him, her, us,* and *them* are **object**ive pronouns, used as **objects**.

"That report gave John and I a chance to redeem ourselves."
Gave *I* a chance? Nope.

"That report gave John and *me* a chance to redeem ourselves."
Gave *me* a chance. Me is the object of "gave."

Pronouns as Objects of Prepositions

Sometimes an error becomes so ubiquitous that incorrect usage begins to sound normal. Consider the "I/she/he" error with prepositions. To understand how prepositions and pronouns work together, remember that prepositions *always* take objective pronouns.

Clue: *for, of,* and *to* are prepositions.

In a radio interview, a best-selling writer said, "It was a big thing for my wife and I to take the plunge."

For I? Would you ever say, "It was a big thing *for I* to take the plunge"? I thought not. It sounds wrong. Please, dear hearts: *for me,* not *for I.*

Or, "Here's a picture *of Sam and she* holding hands." *Of she?* Nope. *Of Sam and her.*

Or, "They said it *to Alex and I* many times." *To I?* A thousand times no. *To Alex and me.*

For, *of*, and *to* cause some of the most common bloopers:

> **for** my wife and **me** (*Not*, **for** my wife and **I**)
> **of** Sam and **her** (*Not*, **of** Sam and **she**)
> **to** Alex and **me** (*Not*, **to** Alex and **I**)
> **for** Alice and **me** (*Not*, **for** Alice and **I**)
> **to** the whole staff and **her** (*Not*, **to** the whole staff and **she**)
> **of** the pirates and **him** (*Not*, **of** the pirates and **he**)
> *or* **of** **him** and the pirates (*Not*, **of** **he** and the pirates)

Here's a heads up on "between":

> **between** us (*Not*, **between** we)
> **between** him and me (*Not*, **between** he and I)
> **between** you and me (*Not*, **between** you and I)

Let my mother's rhyming mnemonic help you: "That's *between thee, me,* and the gatepost."

Prickly Punctuation

Quotation marks (" ")

Periods and *commas* always go *inside* quotation marks.
(" .") (" ,")

Colons and *semicolons* always go *outside* quotation marks.
(: " ") (" " :) (; " ") (" ";)

(Just FYI, this "inside rule" applies in the U.S. It is not the case in Britain.)

Where you put *question marks, exclamation marks,* and *dashes* depends on what you're saying.

If these marks refer to the statement you're quoting, put them inside the quotation marks.

 "Fire," yelled Andrea!

Putting the exclamation mark at the end makes the whole sentence yell.

"Fire!" yelled Andrea.

Andrea has an emergency on her hands. She's the one who's yelling.

If these marks refer to the whole sentence, put them outside the quotation marks.

 Did Woody Guthrie write "This Land Is My Land?"

Reverse the words. Would Woody be asking "Is this land mine?" No.

 Did Woody Guthrie write "This Land Is My Land"?

Putting the question mark at the end, outside the quotation marks, shows that the whole sentence asks about Woody's song title.

Do you know the difference between straight and curly quotation marks? A typewriter used straight quotes (" and '). Today we use straight quotes for feet and inches: 7' 5" Curly quotes (also called smart quotes) enclose direct quotations and dialogue. Can you spot what's wrong here?

 "I'll never tell," said Theo.

Whoops! The direction of the beginning and ending quotation marks is switched. Think of curly quotation marks as numbers—**66** (for start of quote) and **99** (for end of quote). In Theo's sentence, the left and right marks are reversed: 99 and 66.

 "I'll never tell," said Theo.

Here, the left and right marks sandwich the dialogue correctly: 66 and 99.

FAQ _____

You: What's the difference between hyphens and dashes?
Me: Hyphens (-) link words together: smoke-free airport, Ms. Foster-Rodriguez

Dashes are informal. They set off single words, phrases, or clauses.

Use em dashes (—) with words: "Wait—what's that noise?"

Use en dashes (-) with numbers: 39 – 17 = 22; WWII, 1941–45

Exclamation marks (!)

Note how the pros use exclamation points in the books you read.

This many is not okay!!!!!

Stick with one exclamation point. (Perhaps one per manuscript if truly warranted. Unless there's a lot of shouting or noise.)

Plurals versus Possessives

Ever see a sign like this? "Bouquet's $7"
Plurals don't have apostrophes. Bouquets to you for knowing that.
Plurals of compound nouns are tricky. Pluralize the most important word:

> one son-in-law, but two sons-in-law (*Not,* son-in-laws)
> one chief-of-staff, but two chiefs-of-staff (*Not,* chief-of-staffs)

Verbs

Present Tense: A Third-Person Singular Tip

The present tense represents now, this very moment in time.
In the present tense, verbs for the third person — he, she, and it — end in *-s*.

Chester run for home base.
That dune buggy zip down the course.

Chester runs for home base.
That dune buggy zips down the course.

Past Tense

The past tense shows things that have already taken place. In the past tense, some verbs are regular, some are irregular.

With regular verbs, just add *-d* or *-ed* to form the past tense: save/saved, walk/walked.

irregulars, you must know the past tense form. Adding *-ed* to "seek" n't work:

"He never **sought** help." (*Not*, "He never **seeked** help.")

Past Perfect Tense

The past perfect tense shows something that happened before another action in the past. Think of it as the deep past.

> Mike **had baked** [past perfect tense] three perfect apple pies that morning. He delivered [past tense] them by noon.

Past perfect verbs are formed with the helping verb "had" plus the past participle of the verb.

> Regular: had walked, had saved, had sipped
> Irregular: had sought, had swum, had begun

(Both *Nitty-Gritty Grammar* guides have lists of irregular verb forms.)

When you're writing a page about something that happened earlier, cue your reader in by using "had" with the first verb to establish the time frame, then skip it.

> I knew [past tense] Mike would win. He **had baked** [we're into the deep past or past perfect—here's the first use of a helping verb] three pies in the morning. Up at dawn, he picked the apples himself, then let me use the paring knife to peel the red skin. I struggled to make one long curled strip like his, but ended up with jagged bits. His quick hands mixed the dough, sprinkled cinnamon and sugar. Now I **savored** [back from the deep past to the past; no helping verb] the small tart, a bonus for me, and watched with pride as he received a blue ribbon.

To use "had" every time you used a verb in the deep past—"had picked," "had let," "had struggled," "had ended," "had mixed," and "had sprinkled"—would weigh this paragraph down. Read aloud, it would sound ridiculous. Note how the word "now" brings us back to the recent past.

Active Voice versus Passive Voice

The active voice is just that—active. Same with the passive voice—it's passive.

With the active voice, the action is done *by* the subject.

> Jess hit the ball.

With the passive voice, the action is done *to* the subject.

> The ball was hit by Jess.

Writers lean toward the active voice. It's clear and direct. This doesn't mean you'll never use the passive voice; just know the construction.

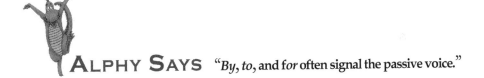

ALPHY SAYS   *"By, to,* and *for* often signal the passive voice."

IN YOUR JOURNAL

Make the passive verbs in these sentences active:

> The flaming baton was caught **by** the majorette.
> The tough exam was written **by** the professor.
> The new Exercycle was delivered **to** the twins.
> The cookies will be baked **for** Mai's birthday. (Clue: Recast this sentence. Who will do the baking?)

Need a quick refresher on these and other conundrums? Judith and I blog monthly as the Grammar Patrol at eFrog Press (www.efrogpress.com). To visit the archives of our grammar columns, visit eFrog Press and click on "Grammar & Usage" under "Blog: Take the Leap" on the main menu.

FAQ

You: How do I copyright my work?

Me: You don't. Once your manuscript is accepted, the publishing house takes care of copyrighting, which is done in your name.

TIP

(For Those with Miscellaneous Brains Like Mine)

Number your pages. Date your manuscripts. Don't even ask about the times in my early writing days my multiple unnumbered, undated printouts spilled to the floor and comingled. Annoying, time wasting. Being a visual person, I now also print various drafts on different colors of paper.

PART II

Get Set!

The Writing Process—From Idea to Submission

CHAPTER 6

Think Like a Writer

In this section you'll get the lowdown on taking your work from start to finish.

But first, in the Monty Python catchphrase, "And now for something completely different": what writers earn.

Get Real—The Finance Factor

Let's discuss the elephant in the room—money. "Don't quit your day job" didn't become a cliché by accident.

Writing for children is not the most lucrative vocation on the planet. The average yearly income for freelance writers in general is not enough to support one person, let alone a family. This goes double for children's writing. Pay is irregular, with royalties usually paid twice a year. Income varies widely—from several thousand dollars to six figures when your books sell well. Dreaming of a big advance? (That's the money you receive from a publisher upon signing a contract; an advance against future sales.) Know that your book sales must earn back every penny of that advance before you'll see any royalties.

That doesn't mean shouldn't wade in. Here's my suggestion: Don't just dream of writing for children—determine to make money doing it. Or at least to begin by covering your expenses!

You may start out with work that's published but unpaid. Look for writing jobs where you can hone your skills as you gain the expertise you need for success. What can you do right now? Write the PTA newsletter? Write travel, how-to, or crafts pieces for your local newspaper? No agent or editor will ever ask you how much you were paid when your writing was published. And, even if there's no pay, you'll get a writing credit for the work. (Hey, letters to the editor count as writing practice.)

Like members of our San Diego SCBWI chapter, your current job may involve writing. Janice Yuwiler writes grants. Wendy Perkins writes for the San Diego Zoo's *ZOONOOZ* magazine (get the free app—too cool). Cindy Jenson-Elliott is the Creative Youth Coordinator at the San Diego County Fair, arranging children's programming for the Youth Tent. Debra Schmidt teaches online classes while continuing to work on her manuscripts. As a result of her biography for young readers about Georgia O'Keeffe, Jodie Shull has interviewed artists and written articles for *Sculpture* magazine. With her journalism background, teacher Grace Nall has written for newspapers, magazines, online, and broadcast media. This expertise made her perfect for writing member interviews for our San Diego SCBWI newsletter. Grace is also an expert in Common Core, hosts Teaching Seasons (www.teachingseasons.com), and writes a blog for teachers.

As a former teacher, I coauthored *Math, Science, and Beyond*, a hands-on family activity program for a local school district. Picture us testing paper airplane models from our desktops, finding how many paper clips can slide into a full glass of water before it spills over, and seeing if watermelons float. We wrote clear, concise directions for hundreds of experiments. We wrote to deadlines. We had our wording of the science concepts vetted by experts. We proofed and produced all the materials. I was paid to work at my craft.

Think, too, of the educational market, particularly if you have a teaching background. After my *Cryptomania!: Teleporting into Greek and Latin with the CryptoKids* came out, I worked with Jan Olsen, founder of Handwriting Without Tears, on a lighthearted workbook for upper elementary students. In *Can-Do Cursive* and *Can-Do Print* (www.hwtears.com) , we wrote pages for upper elementary students on basic cursive, grammar, Greek and Latin roots, and writing. Syndicated cartoonist Jef Mallett, of the *Frazz* comic fame, added jazzy spot art. Schools purchase these disposable workbooks every year. Call this "sideways" writing income, but it's a real bonus when your last name isn't Rowling. I've now written an accompanying workbook, *Greek and Latin Roots for Cryptomaniacs!* for students—a perfect way for schools and homeschoolers to dive page by page into basic roots, with 100 extra roots not found in the book.

You could, like writer Wendy Perkins, have a piece accepted by *Highlights for Children*, get paid for it upon purchase, and have it appear in the magazine seventeen years later.

Make your urge to write more than a hobby. Even if you're not yet published, it's important to keep a detailed calendar and records on all writing-related expenses. Should Uncle Sam come calling, you'll be able to show that you're working at writing by tracking expenses like these:

- Costs of writing classes (dates and receipts)
- Printing and mailing submissions to publishers
- Office supply purchases—toner, paper, envelopes, pens, notebooks, postage, etc.
- Research expenses—mileage on trips to libraries, meetings, conferences, classes, universities, museums, interview appointments, etc.
- Books and other materials
- Travel expenses
- Business cards
- Website hosting and webmaster
- Business phone calls
- Equipment and repairs
- Internet connection

If you work at home, your tax expert can tell you how to report these expenses—if your phone and Internet connection are used for both personal and business, for instance.

I keep records on Quicken; a calendar; and with a Work Overview—a track record of work sent out and pieces published—all proof that writing isn't just a hobby.

TIP

A program like Quicken helps you categorize your expenses. At the end of the year you can print a category report and get a clear picture as to whether you're above or below water, fiscally speaking. Plus, you have a great head start on taxes!

More Truth About Time: Reality

FAQ _____

You: How long does it take between getting an idea and publication?
Me: Unanswerable. You're on your own path.

Split this into two parts. There's the writing. There's the selling.

It's possible that you may whip up a manuscript that sells in short time. The far more likely scenario is that you're in for multiple revisions and a fair amount of hair tearing, teeth gnashing, and time passing. Only then can you set out to get it published.

And do recognize that the first several manuscripts you complete may turn out to be practice pieces only.

If you self-publish, the length of time is up to you. You're in charge of everything from writing through publication and marketing. More info about nontraditional publishing is covered in Chapter 10.

Let's look at trade publications for an idea of how long it takes to get from idea to bookshelf. An average time is two to four years. If a publisher wants a well-known illustrator for your picture book, the path can be long because your manuscript is in a waiting line while the artist completes other projects. From my first query to the publication of *Cryptomania! Teleporting into Greek and Latin with the CryptoKids* was five years. *Water, Weed, and Wait*, about two years.

Since you may have an area of interest or expertise in a specific field, here's the true behind-the-scenes story of two nonfiction books. Judith Josephson and I taught one-day classes in grammar basics through San Diego State University Extension for close to twenty years. The old saw "Write what you know" came to light in a flash when, seven years in, a guy asked after class, "Where's the book?"

Nitty-Gritty Grammar, our first grammar guide, took two years from proposal to publication—time for Ten Speed Press to get the permissions for use of the syndicated cartoons, design a cover, and format pages. *More Nitty-Gritty Grammar* followed several years later. It's more comprehensive, with more grammar terms, an alphabetical format, and some literary terms. It took about two more years.

Now, with one hundred thousand of these grammar books sold, they're "evergreens" — they just keep selling. So identify a need. Put in the work. See what happens.

Your Space, Your Schedule, Your Tools

Where Will You Work?

Find a dedicated place to write. When you're in that space, your brain knows you're there to work. Patricia Reilly Giff's first writing nook was created by her husband. He cleared a closet of the detritus of life and furnished it for her with a flat surface, lighting, and a chair. Boom. She was in business.

Recognize what place (or places) works for you. Do you love to write in coffee shops? Can you write at the library? In the bleachers? At the dentist's office? Or do you need a quiet space?

You do need decent light and a flat surface. Can you make room for writing at your house or apartment? A desk in the corner of your bedroom? An old door on two two-drawer file cabinets in the basement? Need a window? I like looking out my office window at the clouds while dreaming up a synonym for "flighty."

And designate a cupboard, storage bin, or shelves for basic supplies so you're not caught short needing pens, stamps, toner, or a ream of paper at one in the morning.

When Will You Work?

When NPR's *Weekend Edition* host Scott Simon asked Karen Russell, author of *Swamplandia!* and *Vampires in the Lemon Grove*, if she writes daily, she replied, "Sure I do. It's like telling your doctor that you exercise every day. I *try* to write every day. When it's going well, it's my favorite thing to do. When it's excruciating, my favorite thing is lunch."

Russell's wry quote, her titles, and her warm laugh made me want to read her books. This writer has *voice*. She's also telling it like it is.

> *Two important words of advice: "Refrigerator Crispers."*
> *Procrastination is easy. There's always something else to vie for*
> *your attention — even cleaning those pesky refrigerator crisper*
> *drawers. But it takes putting your Seat In a Seat (the S.I.S.*
> *approach), ignoring everything else, to accomplish the writing.*

— Helen Foster James, *Grandma Loves You!*,
Paper Son: Lee's Journey to America, and more
(www.helenfosterjames.com)

There's no single right way. It's one thing to read how other writers go about writing, how they set (or don't set) their schedules. It's another to find your own way of writing. Over time you're going to figure out a writing schedule that works best for you. You have to put in the work to get a finished product. Kathleen Duey jokes that she uses the sash from her bathrobe and ties herself to her computer chair.

More structured: You may work daily, clocking in and out at regular times on a set writing schedule. Some people faithfully write two to ten pages a day (that's a lot). An eighty-seven-year-old I know works daily on her historical mystery from six a.m. to noon. Some writers rise each day at four thirty to write before work. Some stay late at work to write, thus avoiding the rush hour. One new writer squeezes out one morning a week from his busy schedule.

Less structured: Perhaps you'll read all yesterday's work before starting out on today's. Your schedule may be more erratic. You may feel lucky to write on your lunch hour or when the house has settled for the night.

Your rhythm won't be like anyone else's — it will be yours. Many of you are working around jobs, kid or elder care, and other happenings of daily life. You may skip a few days. Just do your best.

Are you a bluebird or an owl? Know what time of day you do your best writing and take advantage of those hours.

You may get clues about your work habits by taking the Meyers-Briggs Type Indicator® (MBTI) instrument (www.myersbriggs.org).

TIP
Try using the MBTI when creating new characters!

How Will You Work?

Quentin Tarantino eschews the word processor for his screenplays. "I can't write poetry on a computer, man," he told the *Los Angeles Times*.

You may go with yellow pads (so portable), then transcribe. You may prefer to work on a laptop in a comfy recliner. The kitchen table could suit you fine for now.

I bend toward paper. Most of my books have begun on scraps of paper or fat yellow pads. I like the pen in my hand and cool ink colors. Once I've keyed in a rough draft, I often print it out so I can go at it with green or blue or purple pens. The mechanical process of getting from brain to hand to page works for me. I can scratch notes in the margins, hack out whole paragraphs, write notes to myself.

But long gone are the olden days when F. Scott Fitzgerald would hand his handwritten manuscripts to Max Perkins, his genius editor, on yellow legal pads. Your final manuscript must be keyed in with standard formatting style. (SCBWI members can learn how to format in THE BOOK, www.scbwi.org.)

Sometimes you'll get into the "zone." You're so immersed in your story that time floats away and you resurface, several hours later.

Sometimes you'll have to force yourself to write. That's where a kitchen timer or iPhone alarm comes in. "Keep going," it says, "until I beep."

Will you listen to music? In an online interview with kids through the New York Public Library, Kate DiCamillo told one reader (she was typing answers—so was skipping capitals!), "i wrote despereaux to bach, winn-dixie to van morrison, edward to rachmaninoff." I click on my iTunes for a Celtic album that somehow signals that it's work time. You may prefer classical or find any music too distracting.

Your job is to find what works for you. All tech all the time? (If so, backups are vital.) A mix? You'll decide how long to keep handwritten drafts once a project is complete. At conferences, classes, and meetings, you can hear how others go about their writing days. Sometimes an idea will click. Take the best of the best and incorporate it into your own writing routine.

Finding Your Style

Think about how Mister Rogers would look you in the eye at the end of each show and say, "There's no one exactly like you. And I like you just the way you are."

Whatever your working style, you'll find it, like it, and it will fit you just the way you are.

"Style" has two meanings: your approach to projects and how you go about working on them; and the way you write—how you put words together—that is, your writing voice.

Discovering Your Approach to Work: How Will You Tackle a Writing Project?

 I tend to write what amounts to an expanded outline for the first draft, and each draft gets longer as I understand more and more what the book and its characters are about.

—Jean Ferris, *Bad, Love Among the Walnuts*
(www.jeanferris.com)

Some of you are highly organized. As you start a new project, perhaps you'll write out major plot points before you begin to flesh them out. You may make tight outlines. Some novel writers fill whole notebooks with sections for character development, plots and subplots, historical backdrop, setting (including flora and fauna), and other details. If you're writing science fantasy or science fiction, you may be creating new worlds, as Jane Yolen did in her Dragon trilogy where the planet has two suns, the herds are dragons, the swear word is "fewmets" (dragon poop), and people will freeze to death if they venture outside after dark.

On the other hand, you may have a general idea of where you're going. Let the words flow and see what happens. Or write an overview of where you're headed, but not be dismayed when a new character shows up or the plot takes an unexpected turn.

One suggestion, no matter what your approach: Make yourself notes on your manuscript at the end of a writing session so you can pick up again easily and not wonder where you were headed or lose a great idea in the ether.

Discovering Your Voice

 Love. Fall in love and stay in love. Write only what you love, and love what you write. The key word is love. You have to get up in the morning and write something you love, something to live for.

—Ray Bradbury (1920–2012), *Fahrenheit 451, Dandelion Wine,* and more

As your skills grow, you'll be exploring and discovering your writing style. Your writing won't have the singular voice of Cynthia Voigt, Rick Riordan, or Jon Scieszka. Those are taken! But by reading widely, you get a feel for what "writer's voice" means. As you devour children's books, notice what styles draw you. Will your writing be literary, poetic, humorous? Try on different styles to see what fits.

You may not use the same voice for each project. Your tone could be serious in one piece, but humor-filled in another.

In that weekly newspaper column I wrote for thirteen years, I struck a casual, upbeat tone—first or second person, contractions, and informal em dashes like these—as if talking to neighbors. Which, in fact, I was.

I've affected different styles in my wide-ranging books. In *Nitty-Gritty Grammar,* Judith Josephson and I used clear, short explanations with lots of specific examples. And my mother may be responsible for my more poetic books. She could whip out quick verses at the drop of the hat for any occasion, from birthdays to new kittens.

It's likely that you may not yet have found your own writing style. Be assured that you will. Give it time.

Goals and Deadlines

Goals

Goals are key to your success. Work out what you want to accomplish. Be clear. "I want to write books for children" is too vague.

Give yourself goals for the week, the month, half a year from now, and a year from this date. A goal for the coming week is something doable: Finish chapter three; go to an SCBWI meeting; prep for critique meeting. A goal for a year from now is big: Complete the first revision of my novel.

IN YOUR JOURNAL

Write goals—small and big—now. Your writing goals can be about any aspect of writing—attending a conference, doing a webinar, taking a class, finding a writing group, getting your printer repaired, updating computer software.

You could start with a goal like this:

> "One month from today, I will turn in my first article or story to a [newspaper, magazine, or contest]." Just fill in the blank.

Check your goals often. Update and refine them. Make this a habit.

Deadlines

Deadlines can be external or internal.
Real (that is, external) deadlines are imposed *on* you . . .

> by a contest due date.
> by an agent or editor.
> by the need to do a final proofing before a book is shipped off to the printer.
> by the chance to have your work critiqued at a conference.

But if you aren't under contract, you may find yourself avoiding writing. If that's the case, set self-imposed (that is, internal) deadlines. No matter what you're working on right now, if you don't have a contract it doesn't mean you're deadline-free. We all need deadlines. Just make your own. Creating your own invented deadline could be all-important for you. It shows you're not just saying you want to write, but are sticking with your goals and actually writing.

IN YOUR JOURNAL

Check your list of potential projects—a nonfiction book proposal, a query for an article on opossums, or that ugly first draft of your YA novel. Give yourself a deadline:

I'll do [your project] **by** _____. Fill in the blank:

- the Ides of March
- my birthday
- by my next haircut
- before my cousin's visit

Jot this invented deadline on your calendar. Stick with it. Need an extra nudge? Put a sticky note on your monitor or ask a writing friend to check on your progress.

Speaking of Dialogue

Stick with "said." Readers' eyes float past the word "said." It's code: "This person is talking. Now that person is talking. Proceed with your reading." This doesn't mean your characters will never utter, screech, sputter, shout, cry, whisper, bellow, or mumble. Just make those times rare.

You can distinguish characters by distinctive elements in their speech. Your eighteenth-century character's speech will be far different from a NASCAR driver's in current times.

Keep it clear. You don't need a dialogue tag for every verbal exchange. Just ensure that your reader doesn't have to go backward to figure out who's talking. Throw in a "said Felix" to keep readers on track. And skim for "said" in books by the pros to see this idea more clearly.

When writing dialogue between students who are moving from French class to geometry, the words will be short, the sentences mere fragments. If writing about a teen who has entered an art contest and is attending a gallery showing for the first time, she's likely to be on her best adult behavior and using more formal language.

Here's a tip from Deborah Halverson for creating believable teenspeak: "Make the conversation about the speaker. Teens are a self-absorbed lot, and that can come out in their words. Frame teen dialogue from a perspective that focuses on how the circumstances affect the speaker. Thus, instead of 'Tom seemed sad today. I wonder why?' use 'Tom blew me off today. What's up with that? What did I do to him?'"

Snoop. Overheard conversations make your dialogue ring true.

The Internet and Common Sense Online

The Internet explodes with information. Dive into children's book resources. Spend fifteen minutes each day learning something more about writing for kids. Use the alphabetical list at the back of this book for clues.

Be discriminating in your use of online resources. If you join an online children's writing group, check out the range of topics covered and the level of expertise. It's best to get advice from the pros, not others just entering the field.

Be alert to sites where the primary purpose for belonging to the group is to self-promote. Or advertise. Or people looking for work in illustrating or graphic design. Or business consultants. Or "I am looking for an agent." Or "We can lift you higher in search engine results." Do you see dollar $igns? Be alert.

IN YOUR JOURNAL

As you explore various sites, jot key points, things you learn, things you love in your journal. Bookmark sites you visit often.

Make Your Own Luck

 Remember the paradox of The Muse: She's not available to you until you've put in so much work that you no longer need her; then she'll fall in love with you.

—Susan Patron, Newbery Award-winning author of
   The Higher Power of Lucky and more
   (www.susanpatron.com)

This next bit may go contrary to the "write for yourself" and "write what you want to write," and "write what your heart tells you to write" vein I've been advocating.

Sometimes it pays to be savvy. Pursue an idea for a book that's needed. (An Alaskan librarian told me kids were looking for books on halibut. Do you know fish? Love this idea? It's yours.) Use your intuition. Avoid what's being published right now. Think ahead.

With *Water, Weed, and Wait*, a San Diego master gardener told us in 2007 there was no picture book for teachers and families to read about kids building a school garden. In August 2010, the book came out. The master gardener had alerted us to the need. We ran with it. (Note that there are now several luscious new books about school gardens and plants, including Rick Swann's *Our School Garden!* and Cindy Jenson-Elliott's *Weeds Find a Way*.)

Carolyn See's Charming Notes

Adult author Carolyn See (www.carolynsee.com) advocates charming notes and writes about them in her *Making a Literary Life: Advice for Writers and Other Dreamers*. (There's a perfect example of the power and importance of nonfiction titles. Inside, you'll find tough, tetchy, hilarious advice. Your eyes will pop and your heart will warm. And yes, author Lisa See is her daughter.)

While teaching at UCLA, See required her students to write five charming notes per week. No expectations of a response. No life stories. No "please read my manuscript" requests. Just a handwritten half-page telling someone—an artist, author, actor, musician, TV or movie writer, TV or movie producer—what you've longed to say: that you loved, loved, loved . . . his illustrations, her characters, his clever script, her movie, her series that makes you laugh out loud and memorize perfect lines just so you can show off, his editorial cartoon.

How do you react when you find a real letter in your mailbox? The same holds for outgoing mail. You'll feel light and right when you stamp and send your own charming notes. Give it a go. The community of children's writers is wide, deep, and kind. Charming notes will help you fit right in.

You never know what will happen. Sometimes nothing. But I've had return notes from advice columnists, cartoonists, *Wait Wait . . . Don't Tell Me!* panelists, newspaper folk, conference organizers and speakers, booksellers, writers, and illustrators. People want and need to feel appreciated. After author Luis Urrea appeared on *Bill Moyers Journal*, we sent Mr. Moyers a copy of *Armando* and told how it had been paired with Urrea's *Into the Beautiful North* for One Book, One San Diego. And wow! Bill Moyers wrote back—a charming, personal letter.

Judith and I met Luis Urrea at a One Book, One San Diego event in Balboa Park.

I confess that I don't always make my five charming notes per week. And I sometimes send charming emails instead.

TIP

Know event no-nos. I was lucky enough to present at a bookstore one evening with Carolyn See. In a wince-inducing moment, a young woman told her, "I've brought my manuscript so you can give me advice." This naïve, hopeful audience member had done no homework, learned no speaker protocol, not adjusted the mirror away from herself to others with questions, or even cracked the author's book on writing before attending. The person next to me groaned aloud.

Writers' Groups

Across the country and around the world, small groups of writers gather regularly to strengthen skills, get input, wrestle grammar conundrums to the ground, get ideas for solving plot puzzles, and support each other.

Your local SCBWI chapter, community college, or library can help you connect with other writers. Look for people who focus on children's writing.

Writing groups aren't for everyone, but I've found mine to be immensely helpful. Besides meeting regularly with others who love words and reading and writing, there are personal perks. If you're deeply discouraged, barraged with rejections, irritated that a book has gone out of print, or just plain stuck, these important colleagues are there to provide a wealth of ideas, insight, and inspiration.

In forming a writing group, set guidelines and standards:

- Where will you meet? When? How often?
- How long will meetings be? How will you divide up the time?
- Will each person read material aloud? Supply copies for all to read from at the meeting? Send material ahead of time to each member? Or will your group consult only by email?
- How often must members read?
- Have snacks and sharing or get right to work?

Think about tough things: What to do when someone doesn't listen to advice offered? What to do when someone rarely reads? What to do about frequent absences? Better to get these issues out in the open than wait until a hitch arises.

Writing groups are patient. I can't tell you how many times my Wednesday group heard *Under the Lemon Moon* as I searched for the heart tug. "It's getting closer," one would say. My Friday group includes both children's and adult writers, so the scope is broader. I value both groups more than words can say.

In both my groups, we have a hard and fast rule: Always, always start with praise:

"I love the part where the girl steps in the gum."
"You really created suspense in that scene."
"The imagery in the attack scene worked brilliantly."
"I could see in my mind what was happening."
"Wow. Your verbs!"
"I love this quirky new character."
"You've made that chapter so much stronger."

Remarkably, each person adds some new insight or hears something others missed. How can this be? To quote Philip Henslowe in *Shakespeare in Love*, "I don't know. It's a mystery."

During a meeting, you need to hear — really hear — what your colleagues say. When it's your turn, you'll get ideas for strengthening and tightening your work to give it the punch it needs to stand out from the slush pile. Absorb all this input. You may not use it all, but weigh how your group's suggestions can improve what you've shared.

Note that protestations of "But that's the way it happened" don't cut it. Here's more from a longtime SCBWI regional advisor and award-winning author:

> *Listen. I mean it! Listen. When others are giving you feedback on your work, keep your mouth closed and listen to what they have to say. As they speak, write everything down — the crazy suggestions, the good suggestions — all of it. Just nod and write. Do not defend your work. Don't break the sacred fourth wall by asking questions in the middle of a critique. Note them down, save them up, then ask them in the end. If a critiquer asks you a question, assume it's rhetorical — unless they show great signs of pain by not knowing, say, the age of your protagonist. Zip your lip. As soon as writers start talking, it turns into defending and then into a nonstop flow of yakking. And when you're yakking, you're not listening. And when you're not listening, you're not learning. Even stupid suggestions can turn out to be worthy of consideration when you reread all your notes in the quiet of your office later on. So listen. And learn. I mean it!*

> —Alexis O'Neill, author of *The Recess Queen, Loud Emily, The Kite That Bridged Two Nations,* and more
> (Websites: www.alexisoneill.com, www.SchoolVisitExperts.com. Blog: www.alexisoneill.com/blog)

Writers Make Connections

Expand your writing world. Try new things. Meet new people. You never know what will come of research, a school visit, a contest you win, a university contact, a writing class, a presentation you do, or an event that feels way out there. Be open to it all.

From the "nothing ventured, nothing gained" department: When Judith Josephson and I were stuck for a strong illustration for "onomatopoeia" while writing *More Nitty-Gritty Grammar,* we emailed Brooke McEldowney, creator of the quirky comic *9 Chickweed Lane.* Six weeks later her strip on onomatopoeia appeared in the paper. *Buzz, hiss,* and *osculate!* Brooke had written "onomatopoeia" on a Post-it and stuck it on her monitor waiting for inspiration. Lucky us.

Connect with others who share your interests. Check out my Pinterest site, Edith Hope Fine, for various writing boards including "Nitty-Gritty Grammar—With a Chuckle," "CryptoKids—Greek & Latin Roots," and "Love These Funnies."

Check out professional organizations. They need speakers for their conventions and will issue a call for proposals well in advance of the conference. A great place to meet new people and get the word out on your books.

The Name Game

Take a hint from Charles Dickens, P. G. Wodehouse, J. K. Rowling, and others. Give your characters great names.

Names can connote age, era, country, and ethnicity. If your book is set in the present day, you're unlikely to find a kid named Edith, Richard, Linda, Patricia, Dennis, Stanley, Elmer, or Edna, unless they're grannies and grandpas. Charles Dickens was a genius at naming his characters. Dip back into some of his books—you'll find Bill Sikes, Scrooge, and Quilip, to name a few. Make it easy for your readers to tell one character from another. Using Sarah and Sally for your BFFs can make readers backtrack repeatedly to figure out who's who. Avoid alliterative or clichéd animal names such as Bucky Beaver, Leo the Lion, a dog named Spot.

Hunting for names that fit your characters? Try these search techniques:

- Google popular baby names by decade or year: "baby names 1947."
- Visit the Social Security site (www.ssa.gov/OACT/babynames) to find baby name data, popular names by birth year, popularity of a name.
- Read obituaries in newspapers or online.
- Try a phone book. (Do you even have a phone book?) Wherever I traveled in the past, I skimmed hotel phone books for first and last names from that region. The best was in Louisiana: Turnipseed. Someday I'll find a home for that surname in something I write.

TIP

From now on—in your reading, in the news, while watching a movie—note pitch-perfect character names. Check how a name sounds when spoken aloud. Is it right for the era? How long is it? Think Huck Finn or Tom Thumb versus Rumpelstiltskin or Ichabod Crane. Antagonists often have snarky-sounding names or with hard consonants: Severus Snape, Voldemort, Darth Vader, Moriarty, Captain Hook, Mr. Hyde, Lex Luthor, Cruella de Vil, Kronos.

CHAPTER 7

Elements of Craft

The Importance of Practice

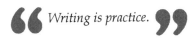 *Writing is practice.*

—Stephen Mooser, cofounder of SCBWI,
Goofball Malone mystery series, and more

In *Outliers: The Story of Success*, Malcolm Gladwell posits that the greats have worked ten thousand hours at their chosen field. Think of geneticist Barbara McClintock, who still worked twelve hours a day in her lab in her eighties. Or a genius like cellist Yo-Yo Ma, who was performing by the time he was five.

Writing practice keeps your writing muscles in shape. As a newcomer to the craft, check out the excellent *What If? Writing Exercises for Fiction Writers* by Anne Bernays and Pamela Painter for more than one hundred different exercises that will help you identify your strengths and weaknesses, with lots of sound advice along the way.

 Spend, at the very least, as much time studying the craft of writing, as you spend studying and analyzing the business of publishing.

—Pam Munōz-Ryan, *Esperanza Rising, Riding Freedom,*
Mice and Beans, and more
(www.pammunozryan.com)

IN YOUR JOURNAL

Estimate how many hours you've spent at your craft.

Surprised? Do some writing right now.

Pre-Writes: Before You Write

We all know the importance of physical exercise. Well, your writing muscle needs exercise, too. When possible, write daily. To warm up, do a pre-write. Pre-writing—techniques to get you into a writerly frame of mind—helps you pull together ideas, grab fodder from the air, link ideas, and get you rolling creatively.

Whether you mind-map, jot a memory, cluster, or journal, you're priming your brain, doing the prep that makes for rich writing.

As a beginner, I was skeptical about pre-writing exercises. The idea of clustering had a slightly magical feel. Then I read the late Gabriele Lusser Rico's *Writing the Natural Way* and tried it. Lo, it *was* magical. And it worked.

Put a circle in the middle of your page. Write one juicy and evocative word (storm, flying, web, garage, illiteracy, underwater, tunnel, spaceship, fear, gold, jungle, etc.), set a timer for two minutes, and let 'er rip. Here is a sample using "storm":

What astonished me most was how, even while spilling out words in a cluster, the brain subconsciously organized thoughts. With "attic," ideas grouped themselves, pouring out in a focused way—one section on sights, another scents, another textures, another of memories, another of feelings brought on by things stored in my grandparents' attic.

Pre-writes are a great way to prime the pump, particularly if you're stuck. You won't use everything in your pre-write, but you'll have fuel to get your writing rolling.

Quick Tips—Honing Your Skills

 If you want to learn good writing, take a chapter or article or picture book and retype it. By typing it, you often see the structure, nuances, and rhythms the author embedded in the text. Then you can apply similar methods to your own work.

        —Patricia Morris Buckley, co-regional advisor, SCBWI
        San Diego, award-winning journalist

By reading this book, you're working on the craft of writing. Here are some specific how-tos that will make your writing stronger.

Vary Sentence Structure

Once, while critiquing a manuscript, I couldn't figure out why it just plodded along—like walking through mud. Interesting plot. Intriguing characters. Oh-ho! I finally twigged to the fact that most sentences started with a noun-verb combo:

> The boys leapt . . .
> The sun blazed . . .
> Hot air balloons soared . . .
> The foxes crept . . .

This is *so* easy to fix. You'll still use the noun-verb form, just add variety. Start sentences with clauses, phrases, gerunds, or adverbs that indicate passage of time (once, later, soon). *Under the Lemon Moon* begins with a rhythmic adverbial phrase: "*Deep in the night*, Rosalinda heard noises."

Vary Sentence Length

In another manuscript the words just sat on the page, as inert as couch potatoes. At last, the discovery: almost every sentence had eight words. Another super-easy fix.

> # TIP
>
> Know when to clip sentences. Cheating? Lying? Fire? Flood? Accident? Dead body? Home intruder? Parent sneaking drinks while chaperoning your prom? If your character is in internal danger or you've reached a crisis point in your plot, shorten your sentences. These clipped bursts of writing cue readers to catch the tension of the scene and pick up their reading pace.

Show, Don't Tell

The first time I heard this "show, don't tell" advice, I didn't get it. Show what? Tell what?

Now I know that "telling" is like watching a TV special on water skiing. "Showing" is like being the water-skier. Telling keeps your reader at a distance. Showing what a character is experiencing plunges the reader into your book.

Show feelings rather than telling how a character feels.

> This tells: Furious, Gerald left the room.
> This shows: Gerald stormed out, slamming the door behind him.

You don't need the telling word "furious" to see Gerald's anger—it's there in his actions.

The subtitle of *The Emotion Thesaurus* by Angela Ackerman and Becca Puglisi is *A Writer's Guide to Character Expression*. To avoid *telling* readers that "Gen was ... (amazed, embarrassed, disgusted, relieved ...)," you'll find definitions of an emotion, plus physical signals, internal sensations, mental responses, and more.

Each page includes a boxed writer's tip, like this one from the "overwhelmed" page:
> "When delivering emotional description, it's easy to rely too much on facial expressions. Instead, look down and describe what the arms, hands, legs, and feet are doing."

IN YOUR JOURNAL

These sentences *tell*. Write sentences that *show*.

> Lexie was worried.
> Yussaf felt overjoyed.
> Grandpa Jordy was exhausted.

Cut Qualifiers

Some words, called qualifiers, modify meaning. They limit or describe other words. Often they don't carry their own weight, like these:

> very really kind of sort of a little bit somewhat rather

Note the difference here:

 Basically, it's a very wise idea to sort of avoid vague qualifiers.

 It's wise to avoid vague qualifiers.

I cut the filler "basically," too—a personal pet peeve. You can cut further:

> Avoid vague qualifiers.

Avoid "That"

> *A big thanks to Dr. Steven Brown, who taught me the danger of the word "that" and who aggressively forced me to write with correct grammar.*

> —Patricia Wood, from the acknowledgements for *Lottery*

Compare:

> Al studied the bronco that he'd worried most about.
> Al studied the bronco he'd worried most about.

ter "bronco" is extraneous. You'll still use the word "that" where
avoid it where you can.

r Verbs

To help your readers conjure up images in their heads, strong verbs are the key.

This sentence tells us little: "Ben went down the block."

Instead of the vague "went," how about if Ben . . .

> leapt   crawled   hopped   raced   skulked   limped   tiptoed   glided

Recast "To Be" Verbs with Stronger Forms

Replace forms of the verb "to be" (am, is, are, was, were) with power verbs.

> *It was* a sunny day.
> The sun *shone* warm and bright.

> *There were* many kids on the playground.
> The playground *teemed* with kids.

Along those same lines, avoid these forms:

> it is   it was   there is   there was   there were

Bag Adverbs

One friend who had developed complex, creative worlds for her science
fantasy novel became enamored of adverbs. She'd string together as many as
four *lusciously, alliteratively, wondrously, deliciously* excellent adverbs. Startled
by the "decrease adverb use" news, she discovered how powerful verbs can
replace adverbs. Now she makes occasional use of a perfect adverb, but relies
on ingenious, specific verbs to carry the day.

Why let go of reliance on adverbs?

> You paint a picture for your readers.
> You power up your writing.
> You shorten your sentences.

> walked slowly = strolled
> moved silently = crept
> talked quietly = whispered

IN YOUR JOURNAL

Replace these phrases with strong verbs:

    ran sluggishly =
    ate quickly =
    moved eagerly =
    stumbled accidentally =
    moved briskly =

Tighten Your Writing

Be concise. Compare:

> We had a gathering.
> We gathered.

> There is a need for the workers to decide.
> Workers must decide.

Finding ways to cut words is fun, sharpens your writing eye, and strengthens your work.

In an early draft of this book, I wrote this:

> Take heed of George Gershwin's life lesson in "It Ain't Necessarily So" from the musical *Porgy and Bess*. Those words apply here.

Now it reads like this (shorter and more specific):

> George Gershwin's famed "It Ain't Necessarily So" applies here.

Use Specifics, Not Generics

Which can you picture more easily?

> A boy sat beneath a tree in the spring.

> Jackson lolled under Aunt Tibby's apple tree. Papery petals, loosed by a spring wind, floated down like warm snow.

(I know. Longer. But far more vivid and visual.)

Engage the Five Senses

Think beyond "sight" — what your characters see and what a setting looks like. Taste, hearing, touch, and scent are powerful forces.

Think of describing a car's interior. You could say "The new car was fancy — nice colors, smooth surfaces." A sentence like that fails to help readers visualize the vehicle.

In contrast, Mildred Taylor's specificity in describing a new car catches sight and touch, plus color and texture, in her brilliant Newbery-winning *Roll of Thunder, Hear My Cry*:

> Inside the Packard, the world was a wine-colored luxury. The boys and I, in the back, ran our hands over the rich felt seats, tenderly fingered the fancy door handles and window knobs, and peered down amazed at the plush carpet peeping out on either side of the rubber mats.

We are in the car with those children, feeling their wonder at the wine-hued interior, the feel of the seats and handle, the sight of the carpet and mats — the sheer luxury. Note Taylor's power verbs: "ran," "fingered," and the alliterative "peered/peeping."

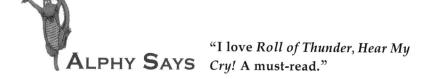

ALPHY SAYS "I love *Roll of Thunder, Hear My Cry!* A must-read."

Scent is especially evocative. While teaching writing to middle schoolers, Judith Josephson and I created an Olfactory Factory as a pre-write. We put things like crayons, mints, a Band-Aid, garlic, a snip of pine, and ginger into zip-top bags and demonstrated how to waft the scents, as in a chemistry lab. For the students, memories flooded in with the scents. After jotting notes, those young writers produced some of the strongest writing of the year:

> "I never told my parents how I skinned my knees when I wasn't supposed to be in the woods behind our cabin. I did my own five-year-old first aid. Cotton stuck and dried in the scab. I still have the scar. Want to see?"

"Was I in trouble. I'd left my favorite purple crayon on the seat of my neighbor's '57 Dodge. He'd spent one long summer fixing, tuning, and restoring that old vehicle in heat and humidity. The horror of discovering the purple melted clear through the fabric set my heart on a bongo beat. I raced for our attic, hiding behind an old leather trunk that smelled of dust and age, never answering when they called my name."

"My Dad grew up in an all-out-for-Christmas family. One year, my Grandpa Jack visited alone. We'd lost Grammy Sue, gone the past July. His clothes bagged in a way I couldn't remember. He stooped. I was even with his chin, not his shoulder. I knew from Dad's frantic decorating he was going all out—lights like *Christmas Vacation,* cider on the stove, gingerbread houses that sagged under the weight of frosting and peppermint candies. We couldn't have guessed how hard Grandpa worked at appreciating that Christmas. We didn't know it would be his last."

Titles and Subtitles

From the start of each new project, work on a title. A strong title can make a difference in sales.

If a catchy title doesn't pop into your head immediately, comb through your manuscript for words or phrases that pop. Stuck? Ask your fellow writers for help. Group brainstorming can yield a perfect title.

Scan titles in publishers' catalogs to know what's out there. Note that one-word titles aren't new (think *Hamlet* and *1984*), but many children's books have just one word: *Matilda, Divergent, Twilight, Holes, Coraline, Stellaluna, Hatchet, Redwall,* and others.

ALPHY SAYS "Titles aren't copyrighted."

Alexis O'Neill's titles shout "Read Me!": *The Recess Queen, Loud Emily, The Worst Best Friend.* Same with Andrea Zimmerman and David Clemesha's playful picture book titles: *The Cow Buzzed, Train Man, Trashy Town.*

Sometimes, the title just comes. *Under the Lemon Moon* felt exactly right and there was no point fooling with it. People hear "lemon moon" and tell me, "I'd like to read that." For all they know it's a lemon cookbook. Or a science book about the phases of the moon. Or a memoir. It doesn't matter. Titles draw people in.

Books don't always have or need a subtitle. But if yours does, make the subtitle focused and specific. Alexis O'Neill's award-winning *The Kite that Bridged Two Nations* is based on a true story. Note her subtitle — *Homan Walsh and the First Niagara Suspension Bridge* — and how much information it packs in. Right away, we have the main character's name and know that this book is about the mighty Niagara Falls. And, hey, the big question: How do you start a suspension bridge over wild, rushing waters, anyway? Note her clever word choice, the book being about a *bridge* that *bridges* (both noun and verb!) the United States and Canada.

Check out some of James Cross Giblin's titles and subtitles:

> *From Hand to Mouth: Or, How We Invented Knives, Forks, Spoons, and Chopsticks and the Table Manners to Go with Them*
> *Let There Be Light: A Book About Windows*
> *Be Seated: A Book About Chairs*

With *Cryptomania!*, I sent my editor a list of potential titles a page long. None rang true. We knew that "Greek and Latin" had to appear in the subtitle and thought "teleporting" would be cool. What's not to love about teleporting? But that grabber title, the *pow*, wasn't there. Brilliant illustrator Kim Doner came up with "Cryptomania." We loved it — it caught how we're both gaga for secrets hidden (*crypto* = hidden) inside big words. The subtitle, *Teleporting into Greek and Latin with the CryptoKids*, clues readers in that it's about friends, zany adventure, and exploring basic word roots.

Nitty-Gritty Grammar's subtitle — *A Not-So-Serious Guide to Clear Communication* — shows that it's user-friendly, not intimidating, and also hints at the chuckle-inducing syndicated cartoons within. People who pick up the book will catch on that it's designed to put grammarphobes at ease.

As you in seek the perfect title for your book, spur your imagination by stacking books from your own shelves. You'll create spine poetry like these from School Library Journal's 2014 Book Spine Poem Gallery.

One perfect gem for writers reads in part like this:

> In Pictures and in Words,
> You Have To Write
> Choice Words,
> Wondrous Words,
> Pyrotechnics on the Page . . .

Chapter Names

Some book chapters are simply numbered. Have you read *The Curious Incident of the Dog in the Night-Time*? Author Mark Haddon gave his chapters prime numbers, so we hop from 1, 2, 3, to 5, 7, 11, and so on. Glorious.

If you decide to name your book chapters, take a cue from Sara Paretsky in her mystery novels for adults, or Rick Riordan and J.K. Rowling in their fast-moving series for young readers. Riordan's first two chapters in *The Red Pyramid* are "A Death at the Needle," and "An Explosion at Christmas." Rowling's first three chapters in *Harry Potter and The Sorcerer's Stone* are "The Boy Who Lived," "The Vanishing Glass," and "The Letters from No One." Who couldn't read on?

Specific, even funny, chapter titles lure young readers into each chapter of your book and remind them of what happened in it. Check to see if you accomplished what you intended. Do the chapter name and the chapter itself fulfill their promise? While you're at it, look hard at the content. Does it move the book forward or is it one you loved writing but needs to be set aside?

Stretch and Grow

When you're brand-new to writing, consider going beyond reading books about writing. How about taking a writing class with other humans? I remember my first class long ago with a great teacher at our local community college. (Good place to start.) Instead of having us turn in our first assignment, the instructor said, "Let's go around and read these pieces aloud." My heart started to samba. I heard nothing others read, and when my turn came, my mouth filled with cotton. My tongue felt dipped in library paste. I wanted to sink under the table. The feedback? They liked what I'd written. They had good suggestions, but their overall response was positive . . . What a lesson. I wouldn't die while working at my craft!

You can find classes from night school to MFA's in writing. Like a few other schools, UCSD in La Jolla, California, is offering a certificate program in writing or illustration for children, with a mix of campus and online classes.

So take that class. Participate. Learn and grow.

Troll through online resources for ways to strengthen your skills. I'm drawn to well-published children's author Bruce Hale's monthly email newsletter, *The Inside Story*. Practical advice. (And zany jokes.) Check out his insightful, free writing tips (www.brucehalewritingtips.com).

ALPHY SAYS   "**Be accurate. Know the difference between Google and a googol.**"

TIP

Can't say it often enough: Back up your work. Save to an external drive, Cloud Storage, a backup program, or a thumb drive. I'll bet ninety-eight percent of you already know this, but I was recently startled when my friend from University of Michigan pointed to the USB port on the right edge of my keyboard. What?! I've been using computers for decades and had no clue.

CHAPTER 8

Put Pen to Paper (or Fingers to Keys)

 You do not know what you can and can't write until you try it. Try it all. Maybe the one thing you thought you could never do will be the thing that breaks you out big.

—Jane Yolen, *Owl Moon, How Do Dinosaurs Say I'm Mad?, Dragon's Blood: The Pit Dragon Chronicles,* and more

The Big Picture

Imagine the credits rolling by at a movie's end. Costumers. Set designers. Props people. Makeup artists. Sound and music and filmography and animation experts. Each person had a job, a focus. But when the movie comes to the screen, all these elements meld into one cohesive, moving whole.

You are your book's *everything*. Writer, director, and all those other jobs. Think cinematically in your writing — compelling action, locations, characters. Take set design, costumes, makeup, and sounds effects into account.

When faced with blank paper or screen you may feel daunted. The task is huge, the path unmarked.

So break the job up. Remember Anne Lamott's *Bird by Bird*. Writing is a process. You'll take it step by step, from idea to final copy, both from the standpoint of getting the words right (the structure, the grammar, the syntax) and the creative places your brain takes you.

From the "Keeping Track" Department

Before I nudge you into actually writing instead of *reading* about writing, a word about tracking your projects.

Writers are creative folk. Organization may not be your highest skill. Here are some strategies to keep you on the right track:

- Keep accurate records. The calendar is your friend: Note writing-related meetings, events, and classes. (Important for you; important for taxes.)
- Track expenses. Keep the smallest receipts—even for a new mechanical pencil. These costs add up. Record your mileage and any money spent when you travel to conferences or do research, interviews, and presentations.
- Keep an overview of your daily work: pages written, calls made, contacts reached, etc., so you can see your progress.
- Write your goals. This makes them concrete.
- Decide on logical computer folders for your writing documents. Some headers may include manuscripts, blog entries, business, speaking, resources, marketing, writing advice, conference notes, finances, contacts, ideas, and blog fodder.
- If filing is low on your list of favorite activities, at least corral each project. I found gorgeous wooden boxes free from a nearby wine-tasting café, useful for clumping lengthy projects or reams of research in one place.
- Once a week, I set my digital timer for one hundred minutes and become my own administrative assistant. Tidy, file, update records, plan the week's To Do list.
- Date everything. Include the date as you name documents. (Valentine's Day 2010 was 021410; and 121212 was a favorite of mine on December 12, 2012). If you experience the horror of a fried hard drive or some other tech disaster and have to get data recovered, you'll know what you wrote and when you wrote it. Or you can be like me. I suffered such a fate. All my data was recovered, but every document was labeled with the same date, November 19, 2007. A cautionary tale for you.

For different versions of the same manuscript, number the revisions: R1, R2 . . . R11. Example: "Scamper Goes Home R7 031714." Some writers put the full year first for easy sorting by year: "20140317 Scamper Goes Home R7" was written on St. Patrick's Day, March 17, in 2014.

Prioritize Your Projects

The more you write, the more you'll deal with multiplying drafts and projects. As you revise, you'll have many versions of the same piece. I love paper and keep all drafts until a book is published. I also keep a computer doc with "leftovers" in the name. There I park sections deleted from various versions in case I need to refer to them later. It doesn't happen often, but I *have* consulted this doc and saved myself from reinvention.

How do you make a decision on what to work on next?

Here's a solution. Create a project overview (OVV) chart. I make a table with these column headers:

Title   Type   Status   Notes   Priority

Title

List each of your manuscripts by name.

Type

Write the genre: MG, YA mystery, PB, etc.

Status

Where are you on each project? Is this just a figment of your imagination? It was a winning contest entry? Do you have one unrefined page? You've completed a rough draft? You've got a final copy? You've tried to sell it? You're stuck?

Notes

Jot down why you started this piece—what drew you in the first place. List critique feedback, your own take as you reread, and any messages from editors or agents.

Priority

Here's the key column. Once you've filled in all your manuscripts, give each one a number from 1 (not much potential; back burner) to 10 (work on this **now**).

Tap Those Ideas

Your idea file has worked. An idea is percolating. You've laid your mental groundwork, read books, taken classes, checked out SCBWI, attended meetings and conferences.

Here's the rub: You'll find no road signs to guide you.

 No STOP (you're going in an awful direction).

 No DEAD END (you've worked yourself into a plot pickle).

 No arrow at the fork in the road to indicate the right path for your story.

But at some point you must write:

 Just do it. Writing, like anything, takes practice and discipline, and I've found that discipline comes from a lifetime of repetition. I started writing when I was twelve and it's made the action as normal as any other activity.

> —Max Brooks, *The Harlem Hellfighters*, and more
> (maxbrooks.com)

How Much Will You Plan?

News: With writing, there's no one right way to proceed.

No one works the same. Some do detailed outlines. Some jot notes or make clusters. Some just leap in. Some use paper. Others plan with computer docs. You'll find your own way.

Even if you plan your novel or nonfiction manuscript, don't be surprised if it changes as you write. Stay flexible enough to go with the unexpected when it occurs to you. It could make your story stronger.

 When you're writing a story, don't think about what other people will think of it or whether it will get published. Concentrate on making it the best story you can possibly write. That's all that counts.

— Betty G. Birney, the According to Humphrey series,
The Seven Wonders of Sassafras Springs, and more

One smart part of planning is not losing ideas. Reminder: Keep a pad or iPad by your bed — inspiration often strikes while you slip off to sleep or just as you wake. Write yourself notes at day's end so your thread or plot point sits waiting patiently for you the next morning rather than wandering off into some irretrievable spot in the basement of your brain.

Your First Draft

 There are three rules for writing a novel. Unfortunately, no one knows what they are.

— W. Somerset Maugham (1874–1965)
The Razor's Edge, The Moon and Sixpence, and more

So true. That's why you need to post a sticky note on your monitor right now:

Write badly to write well!

Grab that fab idea and spit out a draft. It's your first stab at a new piece. Don't be like the writers you see in cartoons surrounded by crumpled pages. Get something down on paper, that all-important first rough draft.

For some, this is easy. They spill words out, page after page, and sit back ready to revise. We'll call them the one percent. For the rest of us, the first stab at a new manuscript can be tough.

Try just blurping the thing out, like those one percenters. Do not go backward. Quash your mental critic's whispers: "cliché," "obvious plot turn," "passive voice," "bor-r-r-ring," or "you call that a transition?"

Write!

Start by writing the parts you want to write. When you get bored or it goes poorly, write something else.

> — Shelley Moore Thomas, *Good Night, Good Knight*; *The Seven Tales of Trinket*; and more
> (Blogs: shelleymoorethomas.blogspot.com, storyqueenscastle.blogspot.com)

TIP

There's no rule about starting at the beginning. Dive into the middle or if that last stunning scene is playing in your head, catch it before it fades away.

Only with this first (very) rough draft in hand can you move to the next key step: revision.

Revision

 I don't think of revising as revising. It's more a question of, "Are we getting somewhere?"

> — Marla Frazee, two-time Caldecott Honor-winning author/illustrator, *All the World, Boot & Shoe, The Boss Baby*, and more
> (www.marlafrazee.com)

The late Peter Matthiessen is the only writer to win two National Book Awards, one for fiction and one for nonfiction. So when he called revision "deepening and distilling," we must pay attention.

The word revision is from the Latin for "look again." Think of revision as pouring strength, power, and energy into your writing. Revision makes your writing sparkle. Makes it stand out from the pack. Helps you find the heart of your piece. Let your writing brain get excited as you move whole paragraphs, cut, sharpen, and clarify, all with your young reader in mind.

Content revision—looking hard at what you've written—takes much longer than that first draft. It's messy, intriguing, hard, puzzling, rewarding. It can be learned.

Prolific children's author Gary Paulsen's first job after quitting the army was editing for a Hollywood magazine. He created a résumé for himself ("my first piece of fiction"), and his three editors soon realized he had zero writing experience. Over the course of a year, they became his teachers, reviewing his work each day. Inch by inch his skills grew.

Now is the time to home in on specific elements in your manuscript:

- Deepen characters
- Tighten plot
- Delete extraneous details
- Cut boring parts
- Reorder events
- Check flashbacks (efficacious or awkward?)
- Eliminate bumpy cadence
- Change "telling" to "showing"
- Press on the five senses
- Ax adverbs by beefing up your verbs
- Read scenes individually for arc and power

 Think of scenes as stepping stones that lead you down the *path of plot.*

> —Nancy Lamb, *The Writer's Guide to Crafting Stories for Children*, and more
> (www.nancylamb.com)

As you've gathered, revision has multiple facets. You'll decide how best to tackle this process—what works for you. Some writers choose to read for one aspect at a time. If you focus on plot, for instance, ask yourself: Do smaller incidents add up to a big climax? Is it believable? Too predictable? Is the tension cranked up? Others writers take the helicopter view—the big picture—by checking on setting, character distinction, and whether the overarching plot is working.

 I'd been published in the academic and professional world and had revised my material three times at most prior to publication. So I laughed when I heard someone say she'd revised her 500-word picture book manuscript seventeen times. I assumed she didn't know how to write. WRONG. Writing for children can be more demanding than writing for adults. The text must be clear, focused, with every word and scene important to the story.

> —Janice Yuwiler, co-regional advisor, SCBWI San Diego
> *Great Medical Discoveries: Insulin*, and more

In an early draft of my *Under the Lemon Moon*, Mamá packed tortillas for Rosalinda to take while she wandered the hills seeking La Anciana. I was taking good care of this sweet girl. If you read the book, you'll find no tortillas or endless hills. Instead, readers hear nighttime noises in the opening sentence on the left page and see the Night Man taking lemons with the first page turn. The second page turn — the next day — reveals her tree stripped of lemons, its leaves turning yellow. Rosalinda faces an immediate dilemma. Readers are plunged into the story.

If you're working on an early chapter book, ensure that each scene moves the plot forward. That dialogue sounds kid-like. That your characters are distinct individuals, not cookie-cutter kids. That there's an emotional tug. That the vocabulary you're using is age appropriate. And whether you've included some laugh-aloud humor that's a perfect fit for your target age group.

With a YA, you may go backward to insert details about a character who wangled her way into your manuscript toward the end. Or check for consistency in time travel details in a complex piece.

If nonfiction, read your manuscript word by word. Check for the unifying theme, gripping anecdotes, and specifics that pull your ideas together. For a newspaper travel piece to get a writing credit, you want readers to see the destination in their minds, long to go there. They should learn something unusual about the place, and get great tips on hotels, food, and attractions. For my Barbara McClintock biography, I had to explain some of her complex discoveries in terms young readers could understand without sacrificing accuracy. Two maize geneticists generously read the parts of the manuscript on genetics to ensure that my explanations were clear and simple enough for sixth graders and up to understand, but still scientifically accurate.

Take time with revisions. With all your changes, be alert to ways to make your writing crisp — avoiding wordiness. I was startled in a writing class when the teacher shrank seven words to two. My "and from there he started out wandering" became "he wandered." Word magic.

Take a tip from William Zinsser, who taught at Yale, as you read through your work. Rather than scratching through parts of his students' papers that might be cut (and cutting his students' writing hearts at the same time), Zinsser used brackets [ ]. He'd put them around single words, phrases, sentences, paragraphs, pages, or even whole chapters to suggest what might be eliminated. He left the decisions to each college writer. Because of Zinsser, brackets have played a key role in my revision.

> **TIP**
>
> After you've put in a good amount of work on your manuscript, let it rest. Put it away for a few days (or weeks!). You'll read with fresh eyes when you return to it.

As you revise, read aloud. It's impossible to stress this step enough. You'll hear bumps in rhythm, extra words, odd syntax, repeats of words and phrases, and those slashable boring parts. Award-winning author Richard Peck rises from his computer to stand and read his words out loud to the empty room. And when you know his books you'll see the genius in that.

Read your drafts out loud to hear how they flow. This illuminating exercise helps you pick up your own writerly tics — a turn of phrase you use too often, or a string of sentences with identical structure. If my manuscript is for a picture book or early reader (likely to be read out loud over and over), I read it aloud at least a dozen times. If I find myself wanting to skip over anything or abridge, that's a place I can tighten.

— Melissa Wiley, the Inch and Roly series, *The Prairie Thief*, and more
(Website: melissawiley.com. Blog: Here in the Bonny Glen, melissawiley.com/blog)

The Mop-Up—Copyediting and Proofing

Once you've completed your content editing and are satisfied with your piece, toss your writer's hat aside, don two nit-picking hats, and switch into copyediting and proofreading mode. You'll do the first clean-up jobs yourself. Prove to an editor that you're the real thing — you have both copyediting and proofing chops.

But don't try to complete this work solo.

Copyediting and proofreading are not the same. Copyeditors focus on formatting, style, and fact checking (an incorrect date, the sun rising in the west, a historical character in a wrong century). Proofreaders catch grammatical and spelling errors that could stop an editor from reading on.

Copyediting

Copyeditors spot factual errors (corn isn't harvested in spring), redundancies, inconsistencies (Steven becomes Stephen), incorrect dates, misspellings of place names, and other glaring slipups.

Even one such error in your manuscript can make an editor reject your work.

If you take the regular publishing route, your editor will tap a copyeditor with high skills. Toward the end of *Cryptomania!*, two different copyeditors cast their eagle eyes over the tiniest details for consistency: Hyphen or no hyphen? Show two forms of a root, or one? Were the page numbers correct for all two hundred-plus entries in both glossaries?

Are you self-publishing? Hire a copyeditor. His or her expertise is worth gold. There's nothing more annoying for readers than finding factual errors, repeats, or inconsistencies in an ebook.

Proofreading

Your last step is proofing — grammar, spelling, punctuation, spacing . . . those telling details.

I've found depressing bloopers in the newspaper recently:

> Its about time. (*Should be*, It's)
> They're many reasons for . . . (*Should be*, There are)
> The professors hat . . . (*Should be*, professor's)
> All writers' know . . .   (*Should be*, writers)

Confession: I fix spelling, punctuation, and pronoun reference errors in library books. With pencil. I laughed aloud recently upon discovering another reader's corrections in the margin along with a smug little happy face. Somebody in the know.

Yes, you should proof your manuscript yourself. Check for these:

- Syntax
- Spelling
- Pronoun reference
- Overuse of adverbs
- Verb strength
- Redundancies (for example, "It constantly changes all the time.")

Eyeball each page. I once realized every paragraph on one page in my biography of geneticist Barbara McClintock started with "Barbara." This was easily fixed by recasting the first sentence of each paragraph.

There's a big difference between trussed and trust! Each time I finished one of my weekly newspaper columns I had to check the whole doc for your/you're bloopers. My fingers had flown. I was on deadline. It's a mistake that can be made in haste.

English has hundreds of homonyms. Your spell-checker has no brain. It won't catch mix-ups with words like these:

accept/except	it's/its
affect/effect	lead/led
altar/alter	lessen/lesson
arc/ark	lightening/lightning
away/aweigh	missal/missle
bail/bale	naval/navel
bare/bear	overseas/oversees
basal/basil	palate/pallet/pallette
boarder/border	past/passed
bridal/bridal	peak/peek/pique
cannon/canon	pore/pour
capital/capitol	principal/principle
carat/caret/carrot	retch/wretch
cereal/seriel	role/roll
chorale/corral	saver/savor
cite/sight/site	sheer/shear
complacent/complaisant	sic/sick
complement/compliment	stationary/stationery
council/counsel	team/teem
creak/creek	tenant/tenet (not quite homonyms)
died/dyed	their/there/ they're
faze/phase	troop/troupe
forward/forword	to/too/two
gild/guild	vain/vane/vein
grill/grille	vale/veil
hall/haul	verses/versus
hangar/hanger	waive/wave
hear/here	who's/whose
idle/idol/idyl	your/you're

Be sure you know the differences between all these sound-alikes.

Don't rely solely on your own eyeballs. You've been so close to your manuscript for so long that you can easily miss tiny errors. Either hire a professional proofreader or bribe a friend who has high proofing skills with an ice cream sundae (or a gin and tonic). While this didn't happen with my *Cricket at the Manger*, I heard about a book whose spine read "Manager" rather than "Manger."

A range of thoughts will rumble through your brain during the writing process:

> Wow. Perfecto.
> Hmmm. This isn't so easy.
> This sounds rotten.
> Yep. It's horrible.
> I'm horrible.
> Why am I writing?
> Wait. Sounding better.
> On a roll!
> Better than ever. Perfecto.
> I love writing.

Know that highs and lows like these are absolutely normal. Be prepared, shrug them off, and keep on keeping on.

CHAPTER 9

Submit Your Work

Your finished piece is ready to send into the world.

Whether it's an early chapter book or a tongue-in-cheek YA horror novel, you've revised, copyedited, and formatted the manuscript exactly right. You've done your very best.

What now?

Target Your Submissions

Be savvy in your manuscript submissions. As mentioned, when you join SCBWI you have access to marketing information that's updated yearly. Check your library for the *[Current Year] Children's Writer's & Illustrator's Market*, also updated yearly, and now with a reasonably priced Kindle edition. While you're at the library, check out *Literary Market Place* (referred to as LMP) in the reference section. The subtitle tells all: *The Directory of the American Book Publishing Industry with Industry Yellow Pages*. Take the time to peruse this volume—a wealth of specific info awaits you.

Do your research to choose which publishers, large or small, look right for your work. Don't even think of starting with the letter "A" of a list of children's publishers and choosing the first ten. This approach won't work. Home in on the publishers most likely to buy your manuscript. Match their sensibility with yours. Talk with children's booksellers and librarians. Get tips from your writing group and at conferences. Really dig to find companies that will be a good fit for your dark mystery, rollicking middle grade novel, or picture book for older readers.

Publishers' catalogues can yield much information. In the olden days we wrote away for writers' guidelines and catalogues, enclosing a buck or two and an SASE (self-addressed, stamped envelope). Today you'll find most houses' lists online. You can also ask children's librarians for older catalogues they're going to recycle.

Learn about the company—its size, how long it's been in business, genres they publish, How many authors and illustrators do you recognize? Check out awards won. Are they a specialty house or broad and general? Some catalogues include subject or theme indexes or, if online, search fields. If you get actual catalogues, note whether it's fat and full color (big bucks; possibly harder to get into) or slim and black and white (perhaps a newer, smaller house eager to discover strong new writers like you).

Writing "To the Editor," "To the Children's Department," or "To Whom It May Concern" on an envelope or letter doesn't cut it. Send your work to a specific person. Find names through blogs, websites, in the dedications of books you love, and, of course, by meeting people at conferences. Who's new at the company? That person is hungry for great writing.

Create a Submissions Chart

Children's publishers aren't one-size-fits-all. Each of your manuscripts is unique. Build an individual plan for each manuscript.

With marketing research in hand, create a submissions chart—as simple as one page per manuscript in a three-ring notebook or a computer document listing at least five publishing houses with the potential for strong interest in your work.

Typical headers:

- Company name
- Editor's name
- Address (or email address)
- Date sent
- Date bought (or turned down)
- Notes

On publishers' websites, find "Writer's and Illustrator's Guidelines" or "Submission Guidelines." You'll learn what to send, how, and where. Some houses only take submissions from agents. These "closed houses" take no unsolicited manuscripts. Skip these for now. Note whether to send submissions by snail mail or email. If the latter, attachments are a no-no for many; they want sample chapters in the body of the email to avoid the danger of viruses.

One House or Several?

Now you're ready to submit your work either exclusively or multiply. An exclusive submission is one sent to only one publisher or agent at a time. A simultaneous or multiple submission is sent several places at once.

For magazines and newspapers, the submission process is straightforward:

- Find and follow the writers' guidelines at the magazine's website.
- Send your piece out.
- Record what you've done on your submissions chart.
- Land on another cool idea and get writing!

If you're sending a book manuscript, the submission process varies.

First, decide if you're sending your work to an agent or a publisher or if you're going to self publish.

Then decide if you're starting by inquiring as to interest or sending the whole manuscript.

Submitting to Agents—The Chicken and the Egg

FAQ _____

You: Which comes first—finding a publisher or finding an agent?

Me: Here's the Catch-22. Many publishing houses only accept agented work. But some agents want experienced writers and may be less eager to represent unpublished beginners.

Getting an agent is challenging for newbies. That doesn't mean you shouldn't try. Here are some ways to get started:

- Use the Internet to find names of agencies and agents.
- Visit many agency sites. Do they actively encourage submissions from new writers?

- Read agent blogs.
- Notice what agents are looking for.
- Find a match for your goals, your style, your voice.
- Chat with agents at conferences.
- Note what genres appeal to different agents.
- Check the lists of writers they represent.
- Find out how long they've been in the business.
- Write a good-to-meet-you note if you meet in person. (Remember charming notes? See pages 87–88.)

You're looking for someone who not only knows the business end of publishing, but is truly compatible with you. Someone who loves your style and has a good eye for ways to make your work stronger before submitting it.

TIP

Don't send your work to an agent in haste. Hold back until you've written a stellar, unique, reader-grabbing manuscript.

Prove yourself. Garner writing credits you can send along with your manuscript to show that others have valued your work.

 When someone is interested in your story, be sure to talk to him/ her before signing anything. Each agent and editor will have a different vision for the final book. It's important that you both start with the same goal. Signing is only the beginning of the real work on your project.

> —Sarah Wones Tomp, *My Best Everything*
> and *Red, White, and Blue Good-bye*
> (Website: sarahtomp.com. Blog: Writing on the
> Sidewalk, writingonthesidewalk.wordpress.com)

TIP

Nail your elevator pitch. Can you say what your book is about in one to three sentences? You may get the chance to pitch your manuscript in the elevator at a writing conference. Some pitches mash two movie titles together: "It's a zany *Christmas Vacation* meets *Home Alone* that boys will love."

Submitting Unsolicited Manuscripts

Submitting your book manuscript directly to a publisher? Consider these ideas:

Target New Editors

New editors actively seek strong new talent as they build their lists. Meet new editors at conferences, get names from fellow writers, or read about these tyro editors online through their websites, blogs, and social media sites. Explore Publishers Weekly's Children's Bookshelf (at publishersweekly.com, search "Children's Bookshelf archive"). You can also subscribe to Children's Bookshelf emails from PW.

Consider Smaller Publishing Houses

Sending your first manuscript cold to a big children's publisher like Scholastic isn't your best move. There's always the chance they'll be delighted with your work, but the odds of doing this are low.

A great strategy is targeting smaller publishing houses. Many consider manuscripts from new writers. They'll publish fewer books each year and their marketing reach may not be as broad, but you'll get one-on-one support from the whole staff when they fall in love with your work. And remember — credits from these publishers count when submitting to bigger houses.

> ## TIP
>
> When you join SCBWI, you gain access to Deborah Halverson's yearly Market Survey, an update on publishing houses. (SCBWI members can log in to find the PDF of the survey in *THE BOOK*, under Resource Library on the website.)

You'll learn:

- Names and addresses/email addresses of editors
- Info on submissions they seek and how they pay
- Names of imprints
- Types of books they publish
- Specific clues. The entry for Lee & Low Books, for instance, notes "Of particular interest are realistic fiction and nonfiction; folktales and animal stories not being considered." You waste their time and yours sending a retold Goldilocks or "Ted Turkey's Tantrum" there.

Query versus Proposal

Studying books' back covers can be incredibly helpful when you're learning how to query. Each blurb is a perfect pitch — to entice you to read the whole story. Notice what is included (the protagonist, the problem, and the emotional drive) and what is NOT included (the details of what actually happens). Master that kind of summary for your own story and you will stir deep curiosity in every agent and editor you solicit.

— Brooke Bessesen, founder and director of Authors for Earth Day, *Zachary Z. Packrat Backpacks the Grand Canyon*, *Look Who Lives in the Ocean!*, and more (www.brookebessesen.com, www.authorsforearthday.org)

Always check author guidelines for the magazine or book publisher before writing a query or proposal. Don't rush these. Take the time to do your best writing. Get input from other writers.

A **query letter** tempts an agent or editor to request a look at your manuscript. A query letter does what it says. It enquires. The gist is this: "I've had an idea. Interested?" Never longer than a page, a query letter is a way to approach an editor with your magazine or book topic.

You'll write a tight description of your idea with focused information on how you'll present it. Give the scope, why young readers will be intrigued, and why you're the one to write it.

Write a strong hook as your lead-in. If nonfiction, include odd/fascinating/striking details. If fiction, briefly sell the editor on your main character and tickle him or her with an intriguing plot synopsis. Skip mention of subplots or minor characters.

In the publishing world, a **proposal** refers to books, not marriage. Do you have a nonfiction book in mind? Sometimes a query letter won't cover the scope of your project. Write a full-fledged proposal to persuade a publisher why running with your idea would be good for the company.

Judith Josephson and I sold *Nitty-Gritty Grammar* on the basis of a proposal. A friend with graphic design skills mocked up a couple of pages with

Thumbs Down/Thumbs Up examples, sample syndicated cartoons, and the ticker tape of common grammatical errors at the bottom of each page. The book ended up with that inviting format.

Elements of a proposal:

Overview

The title, subtitle, an engaging hook and synopsis, why you're sending to this publisher.

Statement of Purpose

Why are you writing this book? What's the goal? Who's your audience?

Your Qualifications

Sell yourself—what makes you uniquely qualified to write this book? Include your social media platforms, speaking experience, other books you've written, and how well they've sold.

The Competition

What else is out there? Name comparable titles and tell how yours is different. Why is your book needed? What makes it competitive?

The Markets

Where will your book sell? Any specific target markets? Who will buy it?

Promotion

How will you help promote the book? Include your experience: You've done well-received national presentations for five years on the topic. You've written a writing blog for ten years and have close to ten thousand followers. Your award-winning books have brought you national speaking engagements. You're active in social media.

Chapter Outline, Sample Chapter

Include a table of contents. Make your writing clear, persuasive, informative, entertaining. (This proves you can do what you say you want to do.) Include research information: a bibliography, people to interview, video and audio links. Choose your strongest chapter and keep it to ten pages or fewer. Double-space everything but the sample chapter. As always, send your best.

Cover Letter

A cover letter accompanies your manuscript. Its purpose is to tantalize an editor and briefly introduce your project and yourself. It anchors your idea and you as a writer.

Include a few lines . . .

- summarizing your piece; a teaser
- telling why you wrote it
- giving your qualifications and mentioning relevant publications you've done

Do mention that you're an SCBWI member, if you've joined. That says that you've taken the time to learn the basics.

Remember KISS: Keep it simple, sweetheart. Always just one page or shorter — preferably the latter.

What Not to Say

Don't point out that the book starts off slowly. If it does and 'picks up on page 42,' put the query letter aside, and start the book where it picks up. You have revising to do. Don't send it yet.

—Stefanie von Borstel, cofounder and agent, Full Circle Literary (www.fullcircleliterary.com)

You know the TV show *What Not to Wear*? Here's what not to say in a cover letter, query, or proposal:

"I've never published anything."

If you're new and have no writing credits, don't mention it. Make your cover letter or query compelling. If perchance you have a specific skill that's related to your idea — you scuba dive or direct a school choir — include that info.

"My third graders loved my story."

These words mark you as a beginner. An editor cares about the strength of your work, not that your class loved it. Your class already loves you. They'll love anything you write! The same goes for your nephew or your friend down the street.

"This is the first in a series . . ."

Those words can be deadly. In your head, you may perceive the manuscript you're sending as the start of a delightful series of books like Betty G. Birney's popular According to Humphrey series, featuring an unsqueakably cool class hamster (www.bettybirney.com). But if you have no writing credits, you're just showing that you don't know how the business works. Publishers want proof that a) you can write, and b) this one book sells before they even think the word "series."

Humphrey has his own Facebook page!
www.facebook.com/AccordingtoHumphrey

Simultaneous Submissions and Rejection Letters

Before you send your cleanly formatted material, let's cover two important topics: simultaneous submissions and rejection letters.

Simultaneous Submissions

Sending one manuscript to several publishing houses at the same time used to be a huge no-no. Nowadays your marketing research will note houses that say simultaneous submissions are acceptable if you inform them.

In my cover letters, instead of the term "simultaneous submission" or "multiple submission," I say something such as, "I'm sending this piece several places at once."

Why note that this isn't an exclusive submission? Because publishing is a business. Even when an editor loves your manuscript, sending you a contract is a big commitment with this bottom line: "Will this book make money for our company and the author?" Remember that staffs have been cut and everyone involved—editor, graphic designer, plus the art, business, and marketing departments—sits in on editorial meetings to make a decision about buying your work. It's a large, lengthy job that involves crunching numbers on costs to buy, edit, design, print, sell, and market your book and still make a profit. If you sell your manuscript to another publisher, but haven't informed the first that it's circulating elsewhere, your name will be mud. Not a professional move.

When I finally nailed *Under the Lemon Moon*, I packed it off to five houses. I got three rejections and a wonderful acceptance call from Lee & Low Books. A full year later, I got a fourth rejection. A point of etiquette: I know now that as a courtesy I should have informed that remaining fifth publisher that *Lemon Moon* had sold. This tale emphasizes again how what's right for one publisher isn't right for another.

Rejection Letters

"Thanks, but no thanks." Anyone who's ever tried to be published has received news like this. To be a writer, you must become impervious to rejection. Make your writing skin as tough as a pachyderm's (*pachy* = thick, *derm* = skin).

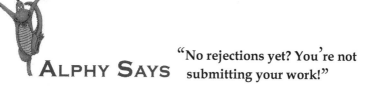

ALPHY SAYS   **"No rejections yet? You're not submitting your work!"**

Madeleine L'Engle had twenty-six rejections on *A Wrinkle in Time*, her Newbery Award-winning classic. Kate DiCamillo spent six years writing and had four hundred rejection slips before she got published. Dr. Seuss's *And to Think That I Saw It on Mulberry Street* was rejected for being "too different from other juveniles on the market to warrant selling."

I sold the first piece I ever sent out, a brief how-to piece for a now-defunct teaching magazine. I got twenty-five big ones. Dollars, that is. *I'm on my way*, I thought.

Then my copy of the magazine came. What a shocker. They'd changed my work. By "changed," I mean they rewrote it. Completely.

Once my heart stopped thudding, I scoured my original submission, comparing it with the (seriously revised) version, noting the *why* and *how* of each change. They'd tightened, rearranged paragraphs to make it more logical, deleted a repetitive section, and pumped up the verbs. In short, I got a profound lesson in editing with invaluable writing insights for a newbie.

Buoyed, I sent out my second piece, a picture book manuscript. Back came a form rejection letter.

Rejected?! How that stung. I took the message utterly personally: "I'm not good enough. My writing is substandard. They don't like me. This is a ridiculous, unreachable dream." I did not submit my writing for another five years.

So listen up. Do as I say, not as I did. Be brave. Be tough. Every writer has been rejected. Onward!

One writer transforms the word "rejection" into "opportunity." Upon receiving a rejection, she tells herself, "Here's an opportunity to send my manuscript elsewhere, to someone who will love it."

Not All Rejections Are the Same

There used to be three general types of rejections you could receive after submitting your work. Now there's a new one. Let's look at all four.

Rejection Type One: The Form Letter

Not that long ago, you might have received a form rejection in your mailbox, returned in the SASE (self-addressed, stamped envelope) you sent with your manuscript:

> "Thanks for sending this. It's not right for us. Good luck sending it elsewhere."
> "Editorial opinions vary widely, so another publisher may feel quite differently."
> "We did not find this submission right for our list."

A few publishing houses still send rejections like these or say the same thing by email. With Rejection Number One, that's it. Don't reply. The agent or editor is not interested. At least you're informed.

Get back to work: more revision, more queries. Send your work elsewhere. Do *not* write back asking why they rejected it. You don't have a relationship with these people. Do *not* immediately send another manuscript. With this rejection "no" means "no."

Rejection Type Two: Note from a Human!

This is also a form rejection, but you may see a note jotted at the end by a real human being. Or an email rejection may include a brief personal note, something like, "Not for us. Try us again." This may seem innocuous. It's not! Someone took the time to write those six words of encouragement. That scribbled note or quick email means something about your research, style, voice, humor, or poignancy caught the attention of a person interested enough to encourage you.

How to react?

1. Don't ignore.
2. Act. Respond.

I've handled "encouraging rejection" like this the old-fashioned way, with handwritten notes. Snail mail. This is not done much today, but it stands out. It's the courteous thing to do and will help the editor remember you and how what you sent appealed to them. Your note will be brief, even a postcard: "Thanks for your encouragement on my [title of your work]. I appreciated your input and will send another piece soon."

If the message came by email, reply with thanks, including the person's original message to you.

Follow through, keeping track of this person's interests on your submissions chart. When you send your second piece, remind the person of the original words of encouragement.

TIP

If your rejection letters contain any personal messages, especially something you perceive as negative, reread them a month later when the sting of "no" has passed. You may be surprised to see something helpful or positive you missed the first time.

Rejection Type Three: The Individual Response

Rather than an outright rejection or a form rejection with a note added to it, you may receive actual input: "We liked your work. Would you consider . . . [here an editor includes thoughts about changes to your manuscript]. If so we'll take another look."

You may get a suggestion about your plot or a way to strengthen your characters. You may be asked to tighten the piece or make a scene clearer.

This is a big deal.

Specific suggestions are gold.

To you, this response may feel like a "non-rejection rejection." There's no guarantee that anything will come of it, but an editor has taken the time to think about your piece and its potential. Obviously, it's your manuscript. You are the one to decide if you're willing to rework it. But any response that isn't a form letter means your foot could be in the door. You've got a nibble. There's interest in what you created. Go for it.

For years, Judith Josephson and I taught "Write Now: Writing for Children" through San Diego State University Extension. Once, as Judith and I covered the different types of rejections, a woman raised her hand. "Oh, I got one of those letters with writing on it," she said. "They wanted me to change two things."

"Is that all? Good! What did you do?" we asked.
"Well, nothing."
"And how much time has passed?" we asked.
"Six years."

Wow. Lost opportunity. That personal feedback about two minor points brought this writer closer to acceptance, but because she didn't realize the importance of the message, she missed out.

If the ideas from the editor strike you as worth trying, get busy. With a minor tweaking, you can resubmit fairly quickly. If bigger changes are suggested, send a note thanking the person for the helpful feedback. Add that you're going to take the time needed to rework your piece, but that you will be resubmitting.

Then don't just think about making the changes. Make them. And submit the revision to the same person, referring to the original suggestions and the date you received them.

You may also get encouragement when your piece is critiqued by agents or editors at a conference. In that case, they may suggest you make the changes then submit the work directly to them. If so, write "requested manuscript" or "solicited manuscript" right on your envelope or in your email subject line. When received, your envelope/email bypasses the proverbial slush pile, giving you a leg up.

TIP

If the message from an editor is neither a rejection nor an acceptance — "We'd like to consider your manuscript if you . . . [fill in the blank]" — take heed. While there's no guarantee of an offer, you're miles closer than you were.

Rejection Type Four: If Not, Then No . . .

Nowadays, in reading guidelines for a magazine, book publisher, or agent you may find this: "If you don't hear from us in [X number of] months, we're not interested."

Translation: "If we're not interested you won't hear anything from us."

This new wrinkle involves no notification, no rejection notice, and is becoming more prevalent as budget decisions put pressure on smaller staffs.

Your manuscript will be shredded or deleted and that's it.

You can counter this "no-response response" by saying in your original cover letter, "If I haven't heard from you in [X months; you decide — perhaps three or four], I'll assume you're not interested." That allows you to keep submitting your manuscript at the end of the time period rather than waiting with bated breath.

In an extra-polite move, you could send a handwritten note, including your name and the name of the manuscript on the envelope. Address it to the person to whom you sent your original submission. Write something brief, like this:

> "I appreciate your taking a look at my [name your manuscript] and wanted to let you know that since my time frame for this submission has ended, I'm sending it elsewhere. I still hope to hear from you."

That could help you cement your name for sending future work to that publishing house. (Because, really, how many people will take the time to do this?)

FAQ

You: I'm getting positive feedback on my manuscript, but the rejections keep coming. Advice?

Me: It's great that someone finds your work strong enough to add comments. If it's just five rejections, forge on with your marketing plan. That's just five people's opinions. If your rejection rate goes higher, take a hard look at your work, analyzing it as an editor would. Read the manuscript through cold, in one fell swoop. Take notes where you spy plot holes, lack of transitions, characters acting oddly, repeats of information, lack of punch. Review the revision section, pages 110–113). It may be time to enlist the help of a pro, someone like Deborah Halverson, (www.deborahhalverson.com) — both editor and author — who can look at your manuscript with fresh eyes.

The Twenty-Four-Hour Turnaround Rule

Keeping track of all your submissions and rejections is vital.

What to do when you think you're close to the end date of the amount of time you've given for a house to review your manuscript? Here's where your calendar and submissions chart (pages 118–119) come in. They'll remind you of the time frame you stated when you sent your work originally.

If time's up for the publisher, assume the answer is "no" and move on (with no moaning, groaning, whining, or fretting; no new submissions to that house). Hop to your marketing plan and get your manuscript back in circulation. If your submission was exclusive, you could now send a brief note stating that while you're still open to hearing from them, you're in the process of submitting elsewhere as well.

The minute you get a rejection, grab your project overview chart and record some notes. Any tips? Any personal notes? Be sure to save names of people who could help you in the future.

If a physical copy is returned to you, check each page. Did a coffee cup leave a ring on page eleven? Are any pages missing? Are they all right-side up? Is this copy clean enough to resend? If not, reprint. When publishers accept email submissions, follow their guidelines precisely; reread your manuscript for errors before sending it out again.

You know the drill. New error-free cover letter addressed to the second editor on your chart. New envelope. SASE if needed. Postage. If submitting again by email, be sure to insert a new editor's name and publishing house; scan for errors before hitting "send."

Presto! Less than twenty-four hours after your manuscript is returned, it's back in circulation. No angst. No hand-wringing. Just a professional move on your part to keep your work in circulation.

Never EVER give up hope. When I created my first Penguin book, I was at a low point – feeling I'd never sell another thing. I'd sold many novelty and concept books in the past when the economy was stronger, but before Penguin's *sale, I'd had rejection after rejection on my favorite projects. I was deeply discouraged. Then the offer came. And another.* Penguin and Pinecone *was sold at auction in a two-book deal with Walker Books for Young Readers (Bloomsbury) in 2011. Two more Penguin books followed quickly. Now I've signed to write and illustrate the fifth book in the Penguin series along with a new picture book series and early readers. It took just ONE idea, one character, one story. Write your next story. You never know if it will be the ONE!*

—Salina Yoon, *Penguin and Pinecone, Found,* and more
(www.salinayoon.com)

TIP

Be realistic. Few manuscripts are bought word for word, as is. Once your manuscript is accepted, you and your editor will continue the revision process.

FAQ

You: How many times do you have to submit a story prior to accep
Me: There's no magic number. This varies widely author to author
manuscript to manuscript.

Rejection Recap

Rejection hits especially hard when you're new. But quitting after one rejection, as I did? That won't fly if you want to make it in the writing business. Learn from me. I do not want to hear that you stopped writing for half a decade because you received one negative form letter.

Let's summarize, so you're reminded that rejection happens. Handle it like a pro. Join the ranks of published writers — give rejection a go! Don't take it personally — a publishing house may be working on a similar piece; the topic may not strike them; the style may not appeal. A fat heap of rejections means you're trying.

On the other hand, it's easy to be rejected. Just follow these rules:

Eleven Ways to Ensure Rejection

1. Include a moral.
2. Submit a seventeen-page, single-spaced, picture book manuscript.
3. Make your nonfiction sound encyclopedic.
4. Talk down to your readers.
5. Use loads of adverbs — they're *frightfully* important.
6. Rely on "to be" verbs: am, is, are, was, were . . .
7. Don't proofread.
8. Ignore the suggestions of your writing group.
9. Make all your characters sound the same.
10. Write forced, awkward rhyme.
11. Above all, do no market research. Send your manuscripts out helter-skelter.

Key Points Thus Far

Since you've reached this point in the book, I'll bet you could give a friend who is new to the field five solid bits of advice on writing for children without peeking at the list on the next page.

IN YOUR JOURNAL

We've covered a lot of ground, both magical and mundane. Take a moment now to go over what you've learned so far and what you've recorded in your journal.

Review points like these:

- Don't wait: Begin writing now. Today.
- Enter a contest.
- Write a piece for my local paper.
- Find my nearest SCBWI chapter.
- Connect with other writers.
- Take classes.
- Attend conferences.
- Send only my best work.
- Illustrations? Not my job.
- Rejections? Learn and press on.

ALPHY SAYS "Your work can't sell from your desk drawer."

The Final, Final Copy

You have to finish things – that's how you learn. You learn by finishing things.

— Neil Gaiman, *The Ocean at the End of the Lane: A Novel,*
American Gods, and more
(www.neilgaiman.com)

Neil Gaiman is right. At some point you must pronounce your manuscript finished and ready to send into the world. When you've done your best, whether it's been months or years, you're ready for the final stages of manuscript prep.

You have about thirty seconds for your manuscript to tap dance on an editor's desk. Your work should be so well conceived and executed that it's like a cork, wafting lightly above the largely unpublishable work that comes in over the transom. (Reminder: The terms "over the transom" and "slush pile" refer to unsolicited, unagented submissions.)

Publishers get hundreds of submissions a year. Way more than they could possibly buy. Sometimes first readers eliminate the least publishable. Sometimes the whole staff has monthly pizza parties and attacks the towering stacks. They're mining for gems. They're delighted when they discover one.

Remember the scene in *Romancing the Stone* after the Wild West opener? Joan Wilder (Kathleen Turner) types THE END and wanders through her whole apartment weeping and hunting for tissues. Her book manuscript was finished at last. Flawless. Her relief was palpable.

Keep your work in the running with professional presentation. Don't be cutesy by including candy or a trinket or a puppet. Editors are unamused by these tactics.

I'm such an optimist that I always think, "I'm ready to submit. I can get this package together, print the final copy, and send it off in an hour." I've learned the hard way to multiply my time estimate by four. You've got the cover letter to write and proof, the final check of your manuscript headers (with your name, title of piece, and page numbering).

What, exactly, will you send?

Succinct Cover Letter

Triple-check the spelling of names. Kellie or Kelly? Shepherd or Shephard? Allyn Johnston at Beach Lane Books has a collection of wild misspellings of her name and letters addressed to Mr. Allen Johnson.

Beware of replicating an old cover letter originally addressed to Ms. Agnes Gooch at Best-o-Kids Publishers and neglecting to change the name when sending it to Ms. Goldie Locks at Three Bears, Inc. This marks you as an amateur and hurts us all. It's truly slush.

Your A+ Manuscript, Perfect in Every Way

Formatting counts. You must turn in pristine copies of your work. Decent margins, numbered pages, standard twelve-point font, black ink. Reminder: SCBWI members can find a guide to standard formatting in "From Keyboard to Printed Page," in *THE BOOK*, found under Resource Library on the website www.scbwi.org.

Very early on, I sent a manuscript on heavy ivory paper with the letters and manuscript printed with an IBM typewriter in italic font using brown ink. Learn from this ridiculous, uninformed error.

Support Materials

Add only relevant material that will make an agent or editor sit up and take notice. Include only information directly related to the project you are submitting or your writing skills. If you're submitting a nonfiction manuscript based on your work as a scientist in Antarctica, it makes sense to note your expertise. Likewise, add writing awards or your newspaper or magazine credits. (No extraneous material, such as a job resume.)

SASE, If Required

If a publisher accepts snail mail submissions, it's easy to send from home with a postage scale and an assortment of stamps. You can order stamps and find a postage calculator online (www.usps.com). I use a First-Class ink stamp for its satisfying *sklonk, sklonk*. This makes your envelope look official—plus, we need all the fun we can get!

If mailing your submission, leave time for the inevitable printer breakdown or ink loss or jam. Triple check to see that you've left nothing out of the envelope and that the pages are in the right order, then weigh the package, add the stamps, address the envelope . . . details. Take the time to do this right.

If email submissions are preferred, follow guidelines to the letter. Know whether this publisher wants you to use the body of the email or send your documents as attachments (and if so, remember to attach said attachments!). Ensure that the email address is correct, use a clear subject line, and make sure you replaced the previous editor's name with the new editor's name throughout.

You've done it. Lick those stamps for your package or press "send" on your email submission.

Now cross your fingers. Your manuscript is winging its way into the world.

Bravo.

You did it.

What now?

Simple. Begin a new piece.

PART III

Go!

"We'll buy it!"

Contract, Publication, Marketing

CHAPTER 10

First Sale and Beyond

THE Call—"We Want Your Book!"

FAQ _____

You: How are you notified when a publisher wants your manuscript?
Me: Just like Nobel winners, you'll get an exciting phone call.

A sale! Yay! You've had that all-important call from an agent or editor. You've sold your first book manuscript.

In rare cases, a book will go to auction. That means that several publishing houses are interested in the book and are bidding for it. This has happened with two of our SD SCBWI members, Salina Yoon and Sarah Tomp. Here's Sarah's story.

 I tried to sell two novels before writing My Best Everything. *After receiving oh so many rejections and writing blindly – not knowing if anyone would ever want to read anything I wrote – it was an amazing and bewildering feeling to have it go to auction. All of a sudden I had four wonderful publishing houses offering to publish my story. But for me, it was the initial call from my agent that was the best part of the process. She was the first stranger to read my story and say, "I love this!"*

—Sarah Wones Tomp, *My Best Everything*
    and *Red, White, and Blue Good-bye*
    (Website: sarahtomp.com. Blog: Writing on the
    Sidewalk, writingonthesidewalk.wordpress.com)

After the "We love your manuscript" call, what happens once your heart quits thonking, your eyes pop back into your skull, and your feet land back on earth after you absorb this great news?

You'll now be working with an editor. You'll get insights and suggestions from a pro about ways to make the manuscript even stronger. These can range from minor changes — a small section that could be deleted or more detail needed in a couple of scenes — to a full rewrite (or two or three . . . or seven).

The editor may ask you to submit revisions before you land a contract or you may get a contract and then work together with the editor on needed changes.

Sign That Contract

Now you'll receive a multipage contract to ponder. (My *Sleepytime Me* contract is ten legal-size pages long; when single-spaced, the manuscript fits easily on a single page.)

It's your job to read and understand the whole thing. I'm not a lawyer so this section contains tips only, not legal advice. Here they are:

- Read every inch of your contract.
- Ask questions.
- Understand everything before you sign.
- SCBWI members will find basic contract information in the *THE BOOK* (www.scbwi.org).
- Talk with published members in your critique group and local SCBWI.

If your book is a work-for-hire project, your contract will specify your flat payment — the set amount of money you'll receive. You get no royalties with work-for-hire, but you can chalk up a writing credit.

When working with a publisher, you'll be offered an advance against royalties: money you'll receive in *advance* of publication — before your book comes out. This money often comes in halves (two checks — one upon signing and the other upon delivery of the final version of your manuscript; or one half upon signing and the other upon publication). This is spelled out in the contract.

Do understand that once your book is out there for sale, it must earn back the amount of your advance before you begin to get royalties. Even if your book doesn't earn back this advance, it is yours to keep.

A contract will cover nonperformance on *your* part; be sure that nonperformance on the part of the *company* is covered so that if there's a problem, you get your rights back. (I speak from experience, alas.)

Today's contracts cover the rights for all forms of your book: electronic, foreign, film, and more. (Picture it: *Nitty-Gritty Grammar, the Movie*. Har-har.)

TIP

Nothing ventured, nothing gained. Negotiate where you can. Royalty rates vary. Ask for a slightly higher rate. (Most agents will get fifteen to twenty percent of your royalty payment.) Is there wiggle room in the number of print copies you'll receive? Ask for more. You may be able to get a higher royalty rate once ten thousand or twenty thousand copies have sold. Ask.

FAQ

You: Do I need an attorney to read my contract?

Me: I've never used an attorney. Your editor or agent has the expertise to help you understand specifics. Of course, their main concern may be their rights, not yours. If you join the Authors Guild (www.authorsguild.org), you can have contracts reviewed free. If you do decide to use an attorney, find a literary contract specialist.

Post-Acceptance and Prepublication

You'll be amazed (or stunned) by the amount of time that passes between signing a contract and holding the book in your hands.

Besides negotiating your contract and finalizing the manuscript with your editor, much happens in that nebulous period between the final acceptance of your manuscript and your book's official release:

- Copyediting
- Proofing
- Graphic design (cover, font, point size, formatting)
- Jacket flap text and blurbs
- Marketing meetings

- Budgeting
- Publicity plans
- Presales
- Printing of F&Gs ("folded and gathered," meaning unbound copies)
- Printing and binding of the actual books

Most of these responsibilities are handled by your editor and others. You should see a final copy before it goes to print. Read every word. Aloud.

Be realistic. Unforeseen delays can be part of this process, too.

As an author, you have prepublication jobs, as well. Be as active as possible in planning publicity for your book. Make good use of that all-important, six-month window before your book debuts.

Fill out the author questionnaire from your publisher. Use your writing voice if you're asked for anecdotes. Return this form quickly. The information you provide helps your publicist tailor your book publicity.

Contact your local paper. Do you or a friend have contacts there? Use them.

If your book is illustrated, work with your artist on publicity.

Bibliophiles are your audience. Keep your local libraries informed. Offer to read to kids, hold an hour-long writing session for readers, do a lesson on found poetry, link music to your book, or design a presentation for the Friends of the Library.

If your book relates to Common Core State Standards, include the information at your author website and let teachers, principals, and superintendents in districts near you know about your upcoming book.

Your Book Arrives: Celebrate!

You've accomplished your goal—a real book. With your name on the cover.

Your box of author copies will arrive before the official publication date.

Picture yourself holding your first book in your hands. Woot-woot!

Few believe I'm shy. But it's true. Even if you're like me, happy working solo at your keyboard, it's important to relish your success. When a box of new books arrives on my doorstep, I borrow kids from the neighborhood and we jump up and down in glee.

You've worked hard for this moment. Take time to . . .

- Stand in the spotlight.
- Take a bow.
- Let your writing group fete you.
- Send member news to SCBWI and your chapter's newsletter editor.
- Toast with a chocolate milkshake.
- Post a joyful message on Facebook, PIN your cover, tweet on Twitter.
- Blog your happiness.
- Take in the kudos of friends, family, and colleagues.

Do bread and butter notes to your editor, the book designer, and the artist—if illustrations were involved.

Still floating on a cloud? Is this the "happily ever after?" Is that all there is to it? In a word, no. Read on.

Whoops! (There Will Be a Blooper)

Don't sidetrack your readers with mistakes. I'll bet you spot errors while reading.

I just finished an admittedly free Kindle ebook in which the author thanked his editor and copyeditor profusely for their help with the clichéd, error-ridden writing, the gaping plot holes, and the unbelievable character action. Plus "its" was spelled "it's" throughout. Such errors and low quality serve only to irritate and distract readers. Professional copyeditors and proofreaders are worth everything to a writer.

Writing a book that's this egregious won't happen with a strong editor and known publishing house. But errors may still accidentally occur.

In my first book, a work-for-hire called *Python and Anaconda*, a switch in the key of the map moved all the pythons of the world to the Amazon basin and all the anacondas to Asia and Africa. I love maps. I love books with maps.

I spotted this horrible switch thirty seconds after opening the book. Not my error, but dreadful nonetheless. I still picture legions of youngsters doing their science book reports and showing their hand-drawn maps of the world covered with misplaced snakes.

In the very first edition of *Nitty-Gritty Grammar*, Judith and I had a great editor and the copyeditor was an expert. On the very first page we'd mistakenly used "hone in on" (sharpen) instead of "home in on" (zero in on). Four word-and grammar-savvy people and we all missed it. Such errors are startling, but easily fixed in future print runs.

When *Under the Lemon Moon* first came out, the beautiful marketing postcards touted "a story of sharing and foregiveness" with an extra e, rather than "forgiveness."

The advice? Move on. You'll live. Such errors aren't the end of the world.

To Market, To Market . . .

Your job continues after your manuscript is finalized. Gone are the days when marketing departments handled all the publicity for a book. Now you'll work on your own and with the publishing house to develop marketing plans that fit you, your genre, and your book perfectly. What's the real picture?

Book Tour? Unlikely.

With budgets pinched and staffs squeezed, nationwide book tours don't happen as often as they used to. Don't set your heart on doing a book blitz around the country unless your book hits the best-seller lists or gets important awards, as happened to Larry Dane Brimner (www.brimner.com) after his *Black & White: The Confrontation between Reverend Fred L. Shuttlesworth and Eugene "Bull" Connor* won the Sibert Award. This well-researched book takes young readers on an important but lesser-known civil rights journey and took Larry on his own wide-ranging journeys.

Social Media? Vital.

Ask friends and fellow writers to help spread the word through social media: Facebook, Twitter, Goodreads, Pinterest, Tumblr, blogs, and beyond. Create an announcement with an email service provider (ESP) like MailChimp or Constant Contact so you can notify your email contacts all at once rather than in small, time-consuming email batches.

Local Bookstores? Yes, with Planning.

Visit bookstores in your area and introduce yourself to the children's buyers. Once you're invited to be there with your book, be sure the store does pre-event publicity. You do the same. At the event itself, you need to do more than sit at a table pen in hand wearing an expectant smile and waiting to sign books.

Entertain!

At a bookstore gig for *Nitty-Gritty Grammar*, the organizer had done a good job spreading the word, so we had an audience. We did a cartoon-driven presentation in our Grammar Patrol hats before signing. In fifteen minutes, we shared memorable mnemonics and common bloopers and got good laughs using big posters of the funniest grammar cartoons in the book. Although the store had fifty copies of *Nitty-Gritty Grammar* on hand, they sold out. (We had not yet learned to tote extra copies just in case.)

Book Launch? For Sure.

Launch your book with pizzazz. Plan well ahead. Think of activities or giveaways that fit your audience, from youngsters to sophisticated teens. Choose a site that fits your book. Invite everyone you can think of — friends, family, the press, fellow writers, neighbors, other guests. Plan light refreshments, readings, hands-on activities for kids.

Ask yourself, "How can this benefit another organization?" Consider your local Friends of the Library, an animal shelter, a community garden, your kids' preschool, a historical association, or other group apropos to your book. You'll double your press reach and give the organization an opportunity to realize profits from your book sales that day.

Anne Bromley held a festive launch for *The Lunch Thief* at a local café. With help from a friend who knows publicity, she sold many books. Yummy event.

Alexis O'Neill did a big weekend launch with Family Day events for the public in both New York and Ontario at Niagara Falls for *The Kite That Bridged Two Nations*. Note the specifics in her planning:

> *For my Kite book launch, I chose a memorable, easy-to-access location – beautiful Oakwood Cemetery in Niagara Falls, New York, where Homan Walsh, my subject, is buried. I did an invitation-only event with food for V.I.P.s before the public launch. Handmade invitations, sent via snail mail, went to movers-and-shakers in the Niagara Falls community: Angels of the Oakwood Cemetery Association, Niagara Falls Bridge Commission, Niagara Falls National Heritage Area, educators from local schools and universities, plus family, friends, and my editor.*

> — Alexis O'Neill, author of The Recess Queen, Loud
> Emily, The Kite That Bridged Two Nations, and more
> (Websites: www.alexisoneill.com,
> www.SchoolVisitExperts.com.
> Blog: www.alexisoneill.com/blog)

My AAUW pals planned an unforgettable launch for *Under the Lemon Moon*. They sent invitations, let the local paper know, and then went all-out with a lemony tea. Tears sprang to my eyes when I walked in. Everyone wore yellow. Big vases with lemons in the base were topped with bouquets of yellow flowers. Lemon treats ranged from bars and tarts to cookies and cakes. To drink? Lemonade, of course. These friends had set up a signing table and had me say a few words. So caring. So memorable.

Judith Josephson and I had a rockin' and rollin' launch for *Nitty-Gritty Grammar*, riding from bookstore to bookstore in a Cadillac convertible with our giant Grammar Bear, all of us in Grammar Patrol hats. Much waving, laughter, and horn honking ensued, and we hauled the bear in with us for signings. Guy Hill Cadillac here in San Diego generously donated one hundred copies to the downtown YMCA.

Angela Demos Halpin and I held our *Water, Weed, and Wait* launch at the San Diego Botanic Garden. The Hamilton Children's Garden buzzed with energy and planting activities. We did four interactive book readings. Kids sat on a big carpet and when we talked about Mr. Barkley, Angela said, "Show us your grumpy eyebrows." Their comically grouchy expressions almost made us fall off our chairs. We showed plants, like sprouted sweet potatoes and lima beans, and gave away seeds for kids to plant.

For my *Sleepytime Me* launch, I held three "come-in-your-jammies" events. The first was a breakfast buffet at our house. Another was for toddler time arranged by dynamic children's librarian Patricia Williams at the Encinitas Library. The last one was at The Yellow Book Road, San Diego's only independent children's bookstore.

I did an interactive reading, with kids saying the "Yawn around, yawn around the sleepytime (sky, farm, town, house, me)" lines of the chorus. They designed their own pajamas on a coloring page drawn by Salina Yoon. We sang "Rock-a-Bye Baby" to favorite stuffed animals and got photos of these well-loved nighttime friends reading *Sleepytime Me*. I was oh so comfy in my robe and piggy slippers, sent by Alexis O'Neill for the line "Piglets whuffle" in the book.

The children's writing community is a supportive one. Let your local SCBWI chapter know about your launch and ask them to come with friends and kiddos.

TIP

Love and support your local independent children's bookseller—they're the lifeblood of children's publishing. In our state we celebrate California Bookstore Day, thanks to the Northern and Southern Independent Booksellers Associations. You may be the one to start an event like that in your state.

 For me, no amount of online convenience can ever equal the in-store experience of browsing and shopping in a bookstore, discovering new books, authors, topics, interests. It is one of life's great and enriching pleasures.

> —Lin Oliver, cofounder of SCBWI
> *Little Poems for Tiny Ears,* illustrated by Tomie dePaolo; the Almost Identical series; the Hank Zipzer series with Henry Winkler; and more
> (www.linoliver.com)

Your Book Is Out. What Now?

Notify Whom? Everyone!

Announce your book to the world. Use all your contacts. That's folks you know, social media friends and followers, the press, columnists. Ask your publisher to send review copies to specific people—supply names and addresses. Since we used names of friends and family in our *Nitty-Gritty Grammar* book examples, we made sure everyone named knew their page numbers.

Go Onstage? You Bet!

Get speaking jobs. I've done more than two hundred and fifty presentations over the years. Let schools and organizations know your good news and that you're available for presentations. Prepare carefully, practice, have backups with you if you're doing a PowerPoint presentation. Follow the Girl Scout motto: Be Prepared. Get a contact phone number. Say what you'll need—tech equipment, a table for displays. Know where you're going. Ask about where to park and if there's a mic. Using a rolling suitcase. Arrive early. I even throw an extension cord into the trunk, just in case. Keep to the designated time frame.

If signing, take a price list and sticky notes so people can spell out names. Have business cards and information (about you, your website, contact info, book info). Ask for a hand with sales (it's hard to act as both cashier and sign books as the author). Have change with you in the form of small bills. And thank the organizers afterward.

Some schools send out information ahead of your visit so families can buy your books if interested. You can sign books ahead and have them organized by room numbers when you arrive. For such presales, I donate part of the proceeds to the media center.

Make your talks lively and interactive. Share inside info with your audience. Illustrator Hernán Sosa added a dog as a pal for Armando on many of the pages in *Armando and the Blue Tarp School*—something for students to look for. During *Armando* school presentations, Judith and I wave a wand and—"Presto! Chango!"—make the school disappear to help kids imagine themselves in a place with no floor, walls, or ceilings. Young readers think with empathy about what it would be like to learn outdoors with teacher David Lynch on a blue tarp at the edge of a municipal garbage dump.

Keep in mind Alexis O'Neill's advice—"You don't *have* to do school visits. Do them if you're comfortable." Alexis offers a wealth of advice in her "The Truth About School Visits" column in SCBWI's Bulletin. Visit her School Visit Experts site (schoolvisitexperts.com).

It's important for groups to value an author's time and expertise. Expect to be paid for your prep time, travel, and presentation(s), or make sure your can sell your book(s) after your talk. There are obvious exceptions. I've done events gratis for my grandkids' school classes through the years as well as reading at events like Read Across America.

FAQ _____

Typical questions (and, bless their hearts, non-questions) you'll often hear from kids at school presentations:

> How old are you?
> How much money do you make?
> Do you have a turtle? I have a turtle.
> What's your favorite book you wrote?
> How did you make the pictures?
> Why are there zebras on your shoes?

Where do you get your ideas?
I have a dog like Armando's.

And here's a true story from a Q and A session that gave six of us from San Diego SCBWI a chuckle when we presented at a local elementary school for their Authors' Fair:

 For many students a published author is famous. So when they ask if you know Justin Bieber and want to know who he's dating, you quickly direct them back to books that you think Justin Bieber would like to read. Preparation and thinking on your feet are the key.

—Suzanne Santillan, *Grandma's Pear Tree*
(Website: suzannesantillan.com. Blog: Writing on the Sidewalk, writingonthesidewalk.wordpress.com)

Get Quirky? Definitely.

Brainstorm specialty marketing. Where else can you market your book? Think beyond bookstores, libraries, and schools. Catalogues? Gift shops? Museum stores?

When *Water, Weed, and Wait* won a *Growing Good Kids Book Award* from the Junior Master Gardener Program and the American Horticultural Society, it began selling in gift shops at arboretums and botanical gardens across the country.

Even after your book has been out for a while, you can help extend its life. How about an event at your home? We volunteered our small garden one year for my AAUW branch's annual garden tour. We lined the borders of the beds with lemons. I made three copper pipe moon shapes to show how the phases of the moon—waxing, full, waning—spell the word "DOC." I signed a lot of *Under the Lemon Moon*s that day.

Autographing Your Books

Think ahead. How will you sign your book? You can just sign your name and the year. Or you can add a message. If you opt for the latter, make your words fit the project and make what you say meaningful.

After Kim Doner and I spoke at an International Reading Association (IRA) conference, she *drew* Alphy with colored pens as we signed books and added a speech bubble for me to write in! (The IRA is now called the International Literacy Association, ILA.) When autographing *Under the Lemon Moon*, I draw a moon and stars and write "May you read by the light of a lemon moon." I now know that that's a lot of words, especially if there's a line waiting, so with *Water, Weed, and Wait*, I write, "Water, weed, and READ!" Much shorter. *Cryptomania!* gets "[Name,] logophile and bibliophile. Carpe curiosity!" I write with a silver or gold pen in *Sleepytime Me* so it shows on the deep blue of the night sky on the glossy end papers. With *Armando and the Blue Tarp School*, Judith and I write, "YOU can make a difference."

Sideways Fun? Serendipitous.

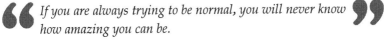

> *If you are always trying to be normal, you will never know how amazing you can be.*
>
> —Maya Angelou (1928–2014), *I Know Why the Caged Bird Sings*, and more

Part of this business of writing for children is just daring. Take a deep breath and reach out in unexpected ways. There's no way to predict what will happen once your book is out there in the world.

Sometimes things happen by chance. You have no control over them. They're frosting on your writing cupcake. Just enjoy the sprinkles on top!

For example, one month KyXy radio here in San Diego named the Spanish version of *Under the Lemon Moon* — *Bajo la luna de limón* — as one of its January Book Club selections for young readers. I didn't even know. A friend alerted me in time for me to contact the station.

My friend Carol, a stellar baker, entered her "Lemony Moons and Stars" recipe in the *Los Angeles Times*' Holiday Cookie Contest in 2012 and told how she baked these delicious lemon shortbread cookies for a tea celebrating *Under the Lemon Moon*. You could have knocked us over with an eggbeater when these moons and stars were named in the top ten. We got to tour the *Los Angeles Times* building and explore the test kitchen. A splashy Sunday article about the top ten cookies and the winners featured a big, delicious photo of the Lemony Moons and Stars. (Sound tempting? For the recipe, visit latimes.com and search for "Lemony Moons and Stars.")

Judith and I were excited when The Park Dale Players, a local children's theater group (www.theparkdaleplayers.com), staged a lively musical production of *Armando and the Blue Tarp School*. The cast of 26 sang and danced; David Lynch spoke movingly after every performance.

Be open to chance happenings like these. And ask your writing group to brainstorm ideas for unusual ways to publicize and market your book.

The World of Social Media

There's a big, fast techno-world out there. Bear these thoughts in mind.

Not everyone is destined to post, favorite (yikes—just verbed an adjective), follow, or re-tweet! If social media is not your thing, don't fret. Not everyone has an online presence.

If you do travel to the social media world, don't try to do it all. Choose the sites that work best for you. Being visual, I like Pinterest. I often find cartoons related to my various writing boards. Posting new items is quick; searches are easy. Be sure to include the URL to your website(s) on each Pin. Follow other Pinners to get traffic to your boards.

Put nothing online (or in email) that you wouldn't mind seeing as a headline in the *New York Times*. I'm not kidding here. Snarkiness, bad language, inappropriate photos, and gossip will follow you forever. Agents and editors do check for your online presence. No grousing about an editor or agent or publishing house. But you knew that.

Don't fall down the rabbit hole and become lost daily on sites like Facebook, Twitter, Tumblr, or Pinterest. Assess what trying to keep up with it all is doing for you. If it's just busywork, cut down your time online. Ditto if it's keeping you from writing. If it's helping you make writing connections or sell your new book, that's fine. Rock on.

As a matter of principle, I don't post photos of children online. The exception: You can post kid pix if you have permission. A friend told me posting her child giving *Sleepytime* Me the thumbs up was okay, but I still didn't include a name or location. At one school, the office had a list of signed parental permission slips saying it was okay to post photos of those particular children online. Otherwise, have someone take a photo of you during your presentation with kids facing you, backs to camera. (Search COPPA online—the Children's Online Privacy Protection Rule.)

If you decide to blog, commit to it. Think of a catchy title. (I love "Writing on the Sidewalk" and "Seven Impossible Things Before Breakfast.") Readers need regular posts—Tuesdays and Fridays? Once a week? Once a month? You can develop your writing voice in a blog and become part of the community of children's writers by spreading the word about lovely new books or events like Children's Book Week or Authors for Earth Day. Do guest interviews. Provide links to cool sites you've discovered that celebrate writing for children.

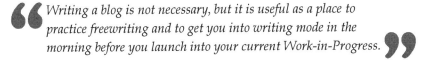

Writing a blog is not necessary, but it is useful as a place to practice freewriting and to get you into writing mode in the morning before you launch into your current Work-in-Progress.

—Wendie Old, *To Fly, the Story of the Wright Brothers*, and more (www.wendieold.com)

Nontraditional Publishing

FAQ

You: I may self-publish. What do you think?

Me: It's an option. But consider this with care. Get the full picture. Decide if this is right for you.

The line between traditional and nontraditional publishing is blurring. Publishing houses are wrestling with their role—from putting a big toe in the water to diving right into the deep end. Many publishers now offer books as both print copies and ebooks, either offering both at the same time or rolling out the electronic version a year or two later. (The *Nitty-Gritty Grammar* guides with Ten Speed Press are examples of the latter.) There have been rare instances when a self-published ebook has been such a hit that a big publishing house snaps up the rights. Check out the path of Hugh Howey's *Wool* and note the rights the author kept.

If you're one of the hearty souls who decides to produce your book yourself you are responsible for the whole deal: concept, writing, revision, editing, copyediting, proofing, cover design, front and back cover blurbs, graphic design and formatting, color palette, font choice, spot art, pricing, ISBN, Library of Congress info, and uploading the final version or storing copies if you go for a print version. If you love juggling nitty-gritty details, you can handle these all these jobs yourself. You can, of course, opt to hire experts to help you write, publish, and promote your nontraditional book.

And you're not finished yet. There are other jobs, like promotion, marketing, selling online, and fiscal tracking — sales, income, and expenses — and mailing copies if you're fulfilling orders for hard copies. You may consider getting a distributor. It's also more challenging to get your work reviewed than with traditional publishing.

Chapter books through new adult lend themselves far better to nontraditional publishing than picture books. If you decide to self-publish a picture book (either hard copies or electronically), add more to the above list of roles you'll play. You'll determine those all-important page turns and acquire the twenty-seven pages of professional, top-quality illustrations that you'll need.

If dollar signs are dancing before your eyeballs, they should be, and said dollar signs are flying *from*, not *to* your bank account! You'll be paying an editor, copyeditor, artist, graphic designer (for cover and interior), and the printer. Weighing costs versus potential income is vital. Get a grip on these expenses before leaping in.

Be sure your manuscript is of highest quality. That's your responsibility. Make it strong enough to be worthy of an SCBWI Spark Award. Even if you publish your book yourself, you'll be signing an agreement with a printer or an online retailer. If you use an e-publishing service, read and understand every word of their contract. Either way, ask questions until everything is clear before signing.

The good news: You get much higher royalties per book.

The dicey news: The marketing is in your lap alone. You'll be designing marketing materials and perhaps buying ads to increase sales.

Your options in the nontraditional route are to self-publish your book, as a hard copy, ebook, or print-on-demand. To decide what's best for you, consider the purpose of your book.

Print Versions

Most self-published print copies are paperbacks. Bound hardcover books are prohibitively expensive.

Photocopies

Are you writing about your own life? Is this manuscript for a golden anniversary celebration? Do your kids and grandkids want copies of the stories you've told them over the years? Think about producing just the number you need.

Get photocopies made on decent-weight paper with the help of your local print shop. A good friend helped an elderly gentleman record tales of his moonshining days in Oregon. Great anecdotes and lots of old photos. His name was on the spine, thanks to the creative help of a kind person at the copy store who printed vertical-word titles on sticky labels for the twenty copies he ordered. There was no expectation of outside sales, but the final product was great for family history. The historical society and the local library also got copies. The former moonshiner was thrilled. It was a treasure.

Print Copies

If you tap your personal skill set and write a specialty book, self-publishing a print copy could work well for you. You know lawn mower repair? Xeriscaping? Growing strawberries? Have lots of tips on playing bridge?

One friend wrote guides to anchorages and marinas for different parts of the country. These are perfect for sailors who need the lowdown on the waters in a given area. We all miss popular local historian Wendy Haskett, but her years of oral history newspaper columns have been compiled into self-published *Backward Glances* volumes, whose sales still benefit our San Dieguito Heritage Museum.

For a limited number of copies you can use an online service like Shutterfly to create a hardcover book with short text and photo illustrations. (This counts in the "Honing Your Writing Skills" Department, too.)

If you want a quantity of books, you can send your finalized files to a printing company yourself or connect with a graphic designer who knows where you can get the best quality at the best price. Be realistic in your print run. Recognize that you'll be storing boxes of your books. Spare room? Garage? Storage unit? When my hardcover book *Cryptomania!* went out of print, I got the rights back and had paperback copies printed myself. It's a slightly smaller size than the hardcover, so fits in a regular manila envelope and weighs less, so I can mail orders from home instead of trekking to the post office.

Print on Demand

Another alternative is print on demand (POD). Books are produced individually when customers want to buy them. When a customer orders a book, the company you've signed up with prints and ships the order. You may get a little less royalty, but you have no storage problems. I chose POD for my *Greek and Latin for Cryptomaniacs!* student workbook, a companion to the book *Cryptomania!*, with three hundred Greek and Latin roots for kids to explore.

Ebooks

We're heading into new territory with ebooks. Who knows what exciting software and design capabilities, unimaginable to us now, will pop up in the future.

While many people still love the feel of a book in their hands, more and more folks are downloading books onto readers or tablets like Kindles, iPads, or Nooks. I often borrow children's ebooks from my county library system. Some school libraries now have the ability to let kids borrow books electronically and even provide the electronic devices. Not surprisingly, even young children are completely at ease with electronic books. (Thus the humor and irony in Herve Tullet's *Press Here* and Salina Yoon's *Tap to Play*.)

Like print books, you can learn how to upload your ebook yourself or get help from experts. While royalties from sales are higher than with traditionally published books, volume is everything. The more you sell, the more you make. But as you know, unless you get outside help, the marketing is up to you.

Some writers turn to ebooks as a way to breathe new life into out-of-print books. That's what we're doing with the Spotlight Biographies series. A group of writers had written strongly reviewed biographies for children that were well researched and carefully edited. When these previously published books went out of print, the rights reverted to us. (We were lucky. Today's contracts cover a publisher's rights to electronic versions.) We are now updating these books through eFrog Press (www.efrogpress.com) with a new cover design and color photos on the pages. We're adding links for young readers to give them easy access to new information, interviews, sights, and sounds. The books are richer for these updates and meet Common Core State Standards for primary research. This new path is exciting. Four sample covers:

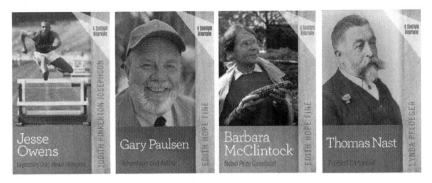

This burgeoning field of nontraditional publishing will shake out over time.

Stats show that more people are reading books today — traditionally published print books, self-published books, and ebooks. In Third World countries, ebooks are growing in popularity. This means more readers. We have no idea what innovations the future will bring, but reading — however we do it — is fine. The world can always use more readers.

Caveat Emptor

From the Buyer Beware Department: If you search online for an agent or publishing info you may be open to "we'll help you get published" pop-up ads. Beware of sites that charge a reading fee. Legitimate agents and publishers never charge to read manuscripts.

Don't fall for sites that say (perhaps more subtly than this), "Pay us. We'll advise you and publish your book." There's an outfit with a number of offshoots operating under many different names seeking to part you from your money. These folks are selling a dream. Lucrative for them, not you. Also known as vanity presses, they just print what you've written. No editing, no marketing, no guarantee of sales. When your fraud-detection antennae quiver, be alert.

If you do consider paying to be published, read every word in the contract. I'd rather see you pay an attorney three hundred bucks to scrutinize and decipher a contract, explaining what each clause means to you, than see you pay a group that offers solutions for writers for "just" three thousand bucks with no guarantee of return on your money. I heard a horrible tale of a new writer who shelled out twenty thousand dollars to get her picture book "published" (that is, "printed"). There's simply no way she earned her money back.

Buyer beware.

The End Is the Beginning

 That's writing for children, eh? We never graduate from first grade. It's a lifelong apprenticeship.

—Anne C. Bromley, *The Lunch Thief*
(www.annebromley.com)

Here you are at the end. This book has given you a boost on writing for children—and lots of specifics to get you started.

FAQ _____

You: Are there really eighty-nine tips in this book?
Me: Nope. More.

Your knowledge of children's writing is now broader and deeper. Your view is more realistic. You know how big and varied the field is. You see how much there is to learn.

And deep inside you know the one true secret to writing success:

Persistence!

And because of my name, I'll add a second:

Hope!

You've longed to write for children. My hope is that you'll keep at it. You'll learn and grow. You'll connect with others who care about writing for children.

I wish you well as you focus on our important audience—young readers from babies to late teens. Your books can be part of their formative years. Your words and ideas can be the ones that influence them for a lifetime. Now it's up to you.

Here's what lies ahead in the days and weeks and months ahead:

- Decisions to make
- Goals to set
- Research to dig into

- Conferences to attend
- Blogs to scour
- Books to read
- Options to explore
- Writing friends waiting to meet you

Most importantly, you have manuscripts to write and send into the world. My friend Jenni Prisk of Prisk Communication (www.prisk.com) trains, inspires, and motivates her adult audiences in nationwide presentations. At the end of each seminar, she reminds her listeners:

> "You have unique skills,
> a unique mind,
> and a unique heart."

You, too, have these qualities. No other writer—nobody—has your exact background. Nobody else's creative outlook and skills are identical to yours.

The writing path you travel will combine *your* life experiences, *your* skills, *your* insights, *your* drive, and *your* imagination.

Remember those three frogs on a log from the beginning of this book? Will you just *decide* you want to write for kids? Or will you make the leap?

The decision is yours.

Two last words of advice:

Jump, froggies!

AFTERWORD

Writing is the first step. You write because you write. Begin by writing for yourself. If writing for children remains your goal, you know what to do: Persist. Grow. Explore.

Thanks, all you new writers, for reading this ebook. I'd love to hear about your first sale. Or your move from articles to books. Or your bold venture into self-publishing. Contact me through my websites (see page 170).

Do you know others interested in writing for the children's market? Please recommend *Jump, Froggies! Writing Children's Books* with its 89+ Beginners' Tips. (Also available as an eBook with live links.)

And, if you're so inclined, hop on over and review this book online. Tell what worked best for you or what surprised you most about writing books for our beautifully diverse audience — young readers. Many thanks.

Write on . . .

Edith Hope Fine

San Diego, California
2015

PS: Remember to think outside the box!
(It works. Four straight lines linking nine dots without lifting your pencil!)

Thinking Outside the Box

MORE TO EXPLORE: RESOURCES
Read, Read, Read to Learn and Grow

Books

Here's a suggested list of books on the craft of writing for you to explore.

(You'll have your own favorites, but this will get you started.)

Bird by Bird, by Anne Lamott

The Business of Writing for Children: An Award-Winning Author's Tips on Writing Children's Books and Publishing Them, or How to Write, Publish, and Promote a Book for Kids, by Aaron Shepard

Children's Writer's & Illustrator's Market (updated each year)

Don't Murder Your Mystery: 24 Fiction-Writing Techniques to Save Your Manuscript from Turning Up D.O.A., by Chris Roerden

Elements of Style, by E. B. White and William Strunk Jr.

The Emotion Thesaurus: A Writer's Guide to Character Expression, by Angela Ackerman and Becca Puglisi

Feeling Like a Kid: Childhood and Children's Literature, by Jerry Griswold

Fiction Is Folks, by Robert Newton Peck

The Giblin Guide to Writing Children's Books, by James Cross Giblin

Making a Literary Life: Advice for Writers and Other Dreamers, by Carolyn See

Nitty-Gritty Grammar and *More Nitty-Gritty Grammar*, by Edith H. Fine and Judith P. Josephson

On Writing: A Memoir of the Craft, by Stephen King

On Writing Well, by William Zinsser

The Synonym Finder, by J. I. Rodale (I love this book. I get lost in it.)

What If? Writing Exercises for Fiction Writers, by Anne Bernays and Pamela Painter

Writing Children's Books for Dummies, by Lisa Rojany Buccieri and Peter Economy

Writing for Children & Teenagers, by Lee Wyndam

Writing Down the Bones: Freeing the Writer Within, by Natalie Goldberg

Writing Fantasy & Science Fiction: How to Create Out-of-This-World Novels and Short Stories, by Orson Scott Card, Philip Athans, and Jay Lake

Writing the Natural Way, by Gabriele Lusser Rico

Writing Picture Books: A Hands-On Guide from Story Creation to Publication, by Ann Whitford Paul

Writing New Adult Fiction: How to Write and Sell New-Adult Fiction, by Deborah Halverson

Writing Young Adult Fiction for Dummies, by Deborah Halverson

Online

The Internet is rich with resources.

Here's a highly unscientific list of Internet sites on the craft of writing for you to explore.

A Word a Day (wordsmith.org)

This daily email is clever, themed, and offers definition(s), etymology, a visual, and lovely quotes. Perfect for logophiles.

The Writer's Almanac with Garrison Keillor (writersalmanac.org)

Receive this compendium of poetry, prose, literary history, and author biographies by daily email or online. A bibliophilic delight.

Blogs about Children's Writing

Start your exploration of blogs by writers, illustrators, agents, editors, and publishing houses. SCBWI members can log in and see the listing in *THE BOOK* at the SCBWI site (www.scbwi.org). You'll find many other blogs to support and enlighten you on your journey. Here is just a taste:

Cynsations
Happy Birthday Author
Here in the Bonny Glen
Picture Book Party
Seven Impossible Things Before Breakfast
The Little Crooked Cottage
Writing on the Sidewalk

International Literacy Association (www.reading.org)

"The World's Leading Organization of Literacy Professionals"
Formerly called the International Reading Association (IRA), this group is now the International Literacy Association (ILA).

American Library Association (www.ala.org)

ALA brings you the Newbery and Caldecott Medals. Watch for the big announcement each January. (Reminder: one "r" in Newbery.)

Publishers Weekly (www.publishersweekly.com)

Keep up with the industry. Get familiar with this site. You can receive regular PW eNewsletters. Enter your email address and check the newsletters you wish to receive, such as PW Tip Sheet and Children's Bookshelf.

Other Online Resources

- Check out university websites on children's literature.
- Find and follow your state's reading association site.
- Trade your favorite online resources with other children's writers
  Being a word geek, I love Rhyme Zone (rhymezone.com) and the Online Etymology Dictionary (www.etymonline.com).

DIG DEEPER!

A Beginner's A to Z Guide to Discovery

There's so much to know about writing in general and children's writing in particular. Check out this unscientific list of topics. You'll now be familiar with many. Explore at your own pace those new to you. Track your discoveries in your journal.

A

advance against royalties
adventure books
agents
alphabet books
ARC, Advance Reader Copy
art
auction
author presentations

B

backlist
backstory
bibliography
bilingual
blogging
board books
book dummy
book proposals
book trailer

C

chapter books
characters
character arc
climax
conflict
contracts
copyediting
copyright
counting books
credits

D

dialogue
didactic writing
diversity
double-page spread

E

early chapter books
ebooks
editing
editors
elevator pitch
endings

F

falling action
fantasy
fiction
first draft
five senses
flap copy
flashbacks
flat fee
folklore
formatting
freelancing
frontlist

G

genres
goal setting
grammar
graphic design
graphic designers
graphic novels

school visits

science

science fantasy

science fiction

second person

self-publishing

senses

setting

show, don't tell

simile

social media

sticktuitiveness!

story arc

storytelling

subgenres

subplot

subsidiary rights

suspense

T

tags

talking heads

tension

theme

third person viewpoint

time travel

tone

transitions

trade paperback

trim size

typography (the fascinating world of
fonts)

U

usage

V

verbs

viewpoint

visits: schools, libraries, organizations,
conferences

voice

W

writing credits

work-for-hire

workshops

X

Come on. What's an X word?

X-cise adverbs and fluff??

X-ray your work before sending?!

Y

YA, young adult

Z

"Good night, nurse," as my mother
would say.

Need a Z or two.

Let's end with a tip of the hat to
two big Zs in children's writing:

Markus Zusak writes deeply felt YA books. If that's your genre, stop and revel in the originality of his remarkable *The Book Thief*. Death as narrator. Unexpected pages of art. A look at a war-torn world with characters who wangle their way into your heart. How could they not? We're all such bibliophiles.

The late **Charlotte Zolotow**, well-loved writer and editor, who contributed greatly to the field of children's literature. Her website—maintained by her daughter, writer Crescent Dragonwagon—says, "Please think of [Charlotte] as standing on her porch and giving you a wave and a smile."

What an excellent way to end a book, with a wave and a smile.

Do good work. Our kids depend on you.

ABOUT THE AUTHOR

EDITH HOPE FINE is an award-winning author with eighteen published books and hundreds of credits in newspapers, magazines, and publications for the educational market. Her books include *Sleepytime Me*; *Under the Lemon Moon*; *Water, Weed, and Wait*; *Armando and the Blue Tarp School*; *Cryptomania! Teleporting into Greek and Latin with the CryptoKids* and the student workbook *Greek and Latin Roots for Cryptomaniacs!*; the  *Nitty-Gritty Grammar* guides; four biographies; and more. She's eager to encourage you new writers who are getting your toes wet in the pond of children's writing and appreciates your online reviews of her books.

For more information visit Edith's websites:

> www.edithfine.com
> www.cryptokids.com
> www.grammarpatrol.com
> www.bluetarpschool.com

You can also contact Edith through social media:

> Facebook: EdithHopeFine/Author
> Twitter: @fineedith
> Pinterest: edithpins
> Email: author@cryptokids.com